# TWENTY-TWO

## WHO CHANGED THE

# WORLD

# TWENTY-TWO
## WHO CHANGED THE
# WORLD

## HAROLD & ELEANOR
# LENTZ

**C.S.S. Publishing Co., Inc.**

Lima, Ohio

Library of Congress Cataloging-in Publication Data

Lentz, Harold H. (Harold Herbert), 1910-
   Twenty-two who changed the world.

   1. Biography.   2. Religious biography.   3. World history — Miscellanea.   I. Lentz, Eleanor, 1910-   .  II. Title.
CT105.L36    1988            920'.02            87-29980
ISBN 1-55673-038-1

# Table of Contents

## Editor's Preface

What are the qualities that make a human life worth noting and remembering? And from whence do they come? Is there a common denominator among those who tower above the landscape?

When I was first privileged to read Harold and Eleanor Lentz's manuscript for this book, those questions tugged at me. I realized that those who eventually rise to greatness may or may not have had the sort of home environment which would seem to give promise of success. Conversely, many who seem to have all the ingredients that make for potential success do not begin to reach the heights.

Why is it some who ought to have become "world-changers" never make an impact, while so many others — not unlike so many in the pages of this book — make heavy inroads for the good?

I think the authors have their finger on the answer. There is something of the sense of the divine, a recognition that there is more to our lives than we ourselves, than circumstances or "dumb luck." The spirit of the person who becomes intoxicated with the knowledge and the urgency of what it is to be a godly individual — that spirit shapes destiny.

Of course, there are far more than twenty-two who could be listed. As I read these brief chapters I made my own list of "the missing whom the authors could have added." But the book would then have been encyclopedic in its scope. There are enough books in the world remembering the lives of many other notables. But these twenty-two may be celebrated as examples of lives shaped for good by godly fervor.

Harold and Eleanor Lentz began this project with the conviction that a life shaped and guided by godliness is by definition vital and successful. If their thesis is correct, then you, gentle reader, when inspired by these twenty-two to "go and live likewise," will change the world by your life too.

— M. L. Sherer

# Foreword

One of the greatest of American preachers, Phillips Brooks, told the story of how he once went with a friend to hear a famous orator. The evening proved to be both profitable and inspiring. As they left the auditorium, Brooks noticed that his intelligent friend had become silent and contemplative. Soon the friend asked Brooks this question about the outstanding speaker whom they had just heard, "Did you see where his power lay?" Thus Brooks was led beyond the evening's enjoyment of a great speech to look for the source of the speaker's dynamism.

This question does rouse one to ask just what there is about some people which enables them to achieve far beyond most of their contemporaries. Where do they find the extra reserves so necessary to keep them striving upward in spite of seemingly insurmountable obstacles? Why do a chosen few live lives of such outstanding accomplishment that their footprints are left indelibly on the sands of time? And, more importantly from a personal standpoint, how can we tap similar inner resources in order to meet worthy goals of our own?

Such questions have led to this study of some of the great men and women of all time, and finally, to the conclusion that while different sources of inspiration, courage and character have led to success, one element in particular appears in many of the lives of greatest distinction. Called by varying names, that element is "religion," "spirituality," "morality," or "faith." Since the beginning of creation, humankind has accepted the reality of a power above and beyond the physical, exerting influence on human beings. Interpretations of that power have varied widely, from belief in spirits and demons among the "unenlightened," to faith in the "God of Abraham and Isaac and Jacob," and in Jesus Christ as the Son of God.

It is true that many people have either ignored or rejected any belief in spiritual forces on earth. But among those professing a faith, there are many who cite their religious belief as the principal source of inspiration for their accomplishments. For the "uncivilized" man, reliance on a higher power was a source of healing, courage, wisdom, and of his understanding of the varied circumstances of life. In our culture the role of religion in the lives of human beings is more clearly enunciated, and has been widely credited as the source of hope, discipline, comfort, guidance, and inspiration.

There is an important point here. One must see that it is impossible to understand fully the history of humanity by confining one's study to politics, economics, or philosophy. Unquestionably, humankind has also been influenced and compelled by religious beliefs. This factor explains the achievements of some of the greatest men and women who have ever lived. Some have openly claimed that their religious inspiration was the cause of their success. Others, while not saying so explicitly, have given ample evidence that this was the impelling force behind their achievements. This has been true among a wide range of human achievers, including intellectuals, scientists, artists, soldiers, and leaders of commerce and industry.

An artist does not work merely with wood, marble, clay or paint and canvas. He must also have unseen thoughts, or themes, which direct his hands in their creative work. The same is true of the architect, as he rears a gothic temple. The poet or essayist, likewise, must be inspired before his fingers produce the words and thoughts that endure. One is reminded of George Washington Carver, the great scientist, who approached his laboratory each day with the prayerful question, "Lord, what do you want me to do with this material today?"

Not only individuals, but whole nations, have been swayed by religion. Its influence has been apparent in their art and architecture, in their literature, and in their politics. There are the deeply religious themes of the greatest paintings in Western culture from Italy, Holland, and Germany; humanity's sacred temples from ancient to modern times — and their spiritual themes which have influenced architecture as well. It is the same in other fields of human interest. Lincoln's oratory drew heavily from his knowledge of the Scriptures; Protestantism laid its stamp on Germany, Scandinavia, and England, Roman Catholicism on Italy, France and Spain, and the Rennaisance and Reformation were eras when religion played a dominant role in the history of nations.

The establishment of the New World was a supreme example of religious beliefs impressing themselves upon a nation of people. Roman Catholicism put its mark on Mexico and South America, while Protestantism influenced North America. From the very beginning of its discovery and colonization, America was destined to be shaped by a strong religious influence. Christopher Columbus was deeply religious. He firmly believed that he was fulfilling a God-given mission when he sailed westward and came to the "New Continent" of America. Therefore, when he landed in the New World, he planted the cross as his first official act, and he called the place to which he had come San Salvador in honor of the Savior. In similar fashion, Cartier planted a cross on the St. Lawrence and read to the natives from the Scriptures. These explorers were followed by a constant stream of missionaries who risked their lives to plant the church in the newly discovered territory.

Later, the little Mayflower brought to our shores a colony of people whose motivation was religious freedom. Upon landing after a strenuous voyage, and upon entering an unfamiliar and dangerous territory, they knelt and "gave thanks to God for his mercies, in their manifold deliverances and . . . prepared to keep the Sabbath." As time passed, all the early colleges and universities of the United States were founded by Churches with deep commitments to the Christian faith and philosophy.

And so, believing that the secret behind the power of many of the most outstanding contributors to human history has been their religious — or spiritual — or moral — strength and commitment, we have set out to study the lives of several "great ones" who have walked this earth — to see to what extent religion was the spark that set them aflame with a desire to be productive, aiding them in their struggles. With one exception, we have purposely omitted all pastors, rabbis, or other ordained spiritual leaders, for it would not be surprising to learn that religious motivations were responsible for their accomplishments. Rather, those included here are the people whose accomplishments were in the secular world. (The one exception is Moses Maimonides, who first excelled as a gemnologist and physician of wide repute, before emerging as one of the greatest religious leaders of Judaism for all time.)

The purpose of this book is to reveal how members of the faith have been inspired by spiritual sources. We have sought as subjects for our study both men and women, ancients and moderns. It is our hope that this publication will help many to see the powerful and positive influence that religion can be in the creativity and achievement of human beings.

Harold and Eleanor Lentz
Lima, Ohio
August 25, 1986

# Alfred the Great

(848-899)

Very few people have so distinguished themselves as King Alfred of England, and fewer still have been granted the title, "The Great," by public acclaim. But such was the case with this Anglo-Saxon who lived in the ninth century. Of his many accomplishments he is best known as the man who freed his country from invaders, (namely the Danes, who sought over a considerable period of time to conquer his dominion). In so doing, he established himself as an outstanding military figure, founder of a navy, organizer of the militia, and fearless leader on land and sea. But great as his accomplishments were in warfare, he would doubtlessly not have won his special appellation if he had not shown talent and greatness in other fields as well. This he did abundantly. So he is remembered, also, as a learned scholar and writer — indeed as the very founder of English prose. He has properly been given lavish praise as a diplomat, an architect, a naval genius, a translator whose works have endured for a millenium, and as the creator of a system of public education.

But, for the purpose of this book, it must be noted that he has been widely recognized, also, as a pious Christian whose faith led him to demonstrate his religion in many practical ways. Alfred is well remembered as a man of deep personal faith who founded monasteries and built churches, and who far exceeded the norm in giving a large portion of his wealth and income to charity.

Alfred came early on the scene as a military figure when, in his late teens, he was called upon to assist his older brother in battles. That brother, Aethelred, held only a short reign before his death brought the barely mature Alfred to the throne. It is remarkable that one who was only eighteen or nineteen could so quickly begin to distinguish himself. The new young king was immediately forced into warfare, and he continued to fight off the invading Danes for most of his life. Finally, after nearly thirty years of intermittent warfare, he at last achieved peace. During that time Alfred gave ample evidence of his military genius, innovation, and strategic skill. So great was his reputation in battle that this factor could have obscured his other accomplishments if they had not been equally outstanding.

Alfred was a voracious reader, and when he tired of that he would have others read to him. He further enriched his mind by committing many poems to memory. Branching out from literature to other fields of learning, he surrounded himself with many scholars of his day. Some were from his own realm, but when he learned of intellectuals in distant lands, he persuaded some of them to establish themselves near at hand where he could take advantage of their knowledge and talents. He himself translated various works, including such outstanding volumes as Bede's *Ecclesiastical History of the English People,* and the creation of Boethius, *Consolations of Philosophy.* He was an author as well as a translator, to the point of establishing himself as "the father of English prose." Before his time, literature was written in the form of verse. It was he who introduced the prosaic form. It can be said without fear of contradiction that Alfred made truly outstanding contributions to early English literature, and his influence has lasted down through the centuries.

An unusually strong interest in matters spiritual and religious, developed at an unusually early age, characterized this great king. He was only five when he went to Rome and, as a young crown prince, was confirmed by the Pope. This visit and contact with the head of the Church awakened an interest on his part in other holy places which he visited from time to time throughout his life, always carrying relics with him in his devotion to the saints. As a pre-teenager Alfred not only read avidly in his mother's church book, *The Missal,* but even astonished his family by memorizing most of it in a short time. As a man, he corresponded with the Patriarch of Jerusalem and established personal contact with other men of devout spirits. His devotional life meant so much to him that he nearly always carried the *Book of Hours* with him wherever he went. It is said of him that he was determined to become the spiritual father and educator of his people as much as their king, and it was to that end that he built monasteries and constructed churches. But Alfred also had a strong sense of stewardship which lead him to give with exceeding generosity to those in need, so that he was a tither several times over.

In drawing up a settlement of peace with the Danes he unashamedly made provision for them to be received in the Christian faith. Because of the many hours he spent in the practice, he was known as a man of prayer. He considered it his duty to know how best to spend his time and money for God and His kingdom. His construction of churches was as a token of his gratitude to God for victory.

Whether by teaching and example, or by threat of punishment, Alfred instilled honesty in his people — so much so that this trait became known in other realms. Here was a king who used his great power not for self aggrandizement, but to guarantee law and order, and to establish justice in the land. He was a model of the moral, God-fearing man, beloved of his people and respected down through the ages as truly deserving of the appelation, "Alfred the Great."

While Alfred is the only king England ever called "The Great," it is significant that other men of world stature also paid him the highest tribute. For instance, Gibbon called Alfred the greatest of English kings. David Hume went all out, labeling him the greatest man in history. Even Voltaire, who did not appreciate religious faith, said of him, "I do not know whether there has ever been a man on earth worthier of posterity's respect." One of his biographers, Alf J. Mapp, Jr., speaks of Alfred thus, "When his kingdom was reduced to thirty acres, he fought back with such courage and genius that he expelled the Viking invaders and made possible the saving of Western civilization. Amazing is his list of other accomplishments: transcendent diplomat, Europe's greatest naval designer, notable architect, law giver, founder of the oldest literary tradition in the Occident, originator of a system of public education, and producer of translations that have endured a thousand years."

Fully to know and appreciate Alfred as a restorer of peace, law and order on a strong moral basis, one has to be aware of the social situations he had inherited when he became ruler of Wessex. His kingdom was almost totally disorganized, and little wonder — it had been subjected to invasions for more than fifty years. In great numbers, the men had died in warfare, buildings had been laid waste, fields scorched. Even worse, human deterioration had taken place under the cruelty of war; people's hearts had become hardened and selfish. To restore and uplift the human

spirit, Alfred compiled a set of laws for his people, aimed at creating not only a peaceful society but one with moral character. In
the introduction to the compilation of his laws, Alfred's religious
emphasis became prominent, for he openly stated that his laws
were, "based upon the Ten Commandments given by God to
Moses; fulfilled and interpreted by the love and compassion of his
Son, the Healer, the Lord Christ; continued in the teachings of
the Apostles, and thence down the ages by synods of the church
and decrees of kings."

In the laws themselves were numerous decrees aimed at
strengthening the religious life of the people. On more than fifty
holy days, other than Sunday, observance was to be noted by
declaring a holiday. Lent was to be a time of emphasis on prayer,
with certain restrictions on daily life. Alfred's laws supported the
church in its long fight against magic and witchcraft by ordering
the death penalty for those who engaged in such practices. All of
this reflected the lasting influence of the Papal blessing bestowed
upon an impressionable boy, only five years old when the Pope
chose to "gird him with the honor and the outward trappings of
a consul of Rome." One can imagine young Alfred's feelings when
the powerful Leo IV robed him in a white and purple cloak, placed
a crown upon his head, and invested him with a sword. Years
later, when he became king, Alfred declared that a successful
monarch must have the trilogy of "praying men, fighting men and
working men," apparently in that order.

Alfred was fifty-one years old at his death, so his tremendous
accomplishments were achieved at a fairly young age. Already at
thirty-eight he could look with satisfaction upon the fact that he
had driven out the marauding Danes, had added Mercia and Kent
to Wessex as his natural realm, had pioneered in military weapons
and strategy both on land and on sea, and had restored a strong
peace by his trading regulations and judicial establishments. He
was so renowned for his integrity that he was called "The
Truthteller," and he was a translator who was so well versed in
Latin that his work made the Latin classics available to his coun-
trymen in their own language. With regard to the development
of the English language, we are told that the special appeal of Chur-
chill, Mark Twain, Dickens, and Shakespeare is all due to the prior
work of Alfred.

The feats of Alfred are the more remarkable when one

considers the fact that he was in poor health throughout his life-time. The exact nature of his illness, referred to as "seizures," is not known. But his friend, Asser, wrote of the king that "he has not a single hour's security in which he is not either suffering that infirmity, or being driven almost to desperation by the fear of its coming."

At the age of 20 Alfred married the girl named Ealswerth, daughter of an earl. They had five children, the oldest, Edward, succeeding to the throne at his father's death. Edward had distinguished himself in battle as a prince and was a promising inheritor of a mighty crown. So Alfred left behind him an heir through whom the spirit of the father would carry on.

Clearly, then, history proclaims — Alfred the Great should be remembered and honored today not merely as a king, but also as a man, and as an example, of phenomenal talents and of sterling character.

# Moses Maimonides
## (Moses ben Maimon)

(1135-1204)

Maimonides is a notable example of a man with singular accomplishments in each of several fields, but for whom religion was the essential, driving force in a momentous career. He was an outstanding physician, a philosopher who exerted a strong influence on some of the greatest minds of all time, a politician, a jeweler, a philanthropist, but above all else, a codifier of Jewish law and the most famous student of that law since the prophet Moses. He is accepted as the foremost intellectual of medieval Judaism.

His early life was that of a wanderer. Cordova, Spain, the city of his birth, was taken over by Muslims who tried to force all inhabitants to accept Islam. Forced to flee, he roamed about Andalusia, trying to keep ahead of the fanatical Almohades who threatened his life. From Spain he went to Morocco where the enmity of the Almohades pursued him. Forced once again to flee, he went to Egypt, where he met with much sorrow from the death of his father, his brother who had succeeded to the head of the family jewelry business, and his son.

Somewhat later, however, Maimonides' fortunes began to improve. Early in life he had prepared himself well, studying rabbinics, medicine, astronomy, mathematics, and Greek philosophy. It was in the field of medicine that he was to first meet with success. Maimonides emerged as an outstanding physician, so capable that he caught the eye of the Sultan. The ruler appointed Maimonides as his personal physician, a position which brought him considerable distinction. Later he would decline a similar position in England when approached by representatives of Richard the Lionhearted.

Much more than a practitioner, Maimonides established a wide reputation through his many writings in the field of medicine. A prodigious writer in many fields, his medical writings covered a wide range of topics, including allergies, epilepsy, the physical constitution, the effect of psychosomatics, and the nervous system. He showed an understanding of medicine far ahead of his time and produced ten books in the field. As a physician Maimonides prescribed drugs sparingly, and then only as a last resort. His primary emphasis was on proper diet, which he believed would help the patient's body to cure itself, and which he detailed in a dietetic rulebook for Saladin. Many of Maimonides' works were being translated into languages other than their original Arabic, and enjoyed wide circulation abroad as well as in Egypt.

As Maimonides' fortunes grew and he became a man of wealth, he gladly shared his means with others — sufficiently so that he could be called a philanthropist. He was especially happy to show hospitality to Jews, and his home came to be a practically free hotel for travelers. Perhaps the chief source of his wealth was the family jewelry business, which dealt principally in expensive gems, a field in which he became an expert.

Maimonides also engaged in the subtle art of politics in Egypt. At times it threatened to be his undoing, but it was also responsible for his elevation to a position of great authority. An exilarchate (a banding of Jewish exiles) had been established in Babylon in about the second century. The line of civil and judicial rulers of the exilarchate bore the name "exilarch." Jews in all countries paid tribute to these religious-political leaders. When the exilarchate for Jews was established in Egypt, Maimonides was lifted to great power by the Exilarch of Judah, who decreed that when Maimonides decided a point of Law the decision was final. Thus, as the greatest scholar in Egypt, Maimonides became the leader of the Jews throughout the Saladin Kingdom. Soon questions concerning Jewish law were sent to him from a number of other nations as well, and Maimonides was recognized internationally as an expert in the field.

In addition to theology, another interest of this multi-talented man was music. He not only appreciated great music and encouraged its acceptance, but was himself a composer, creating congregational hymns for use in Jewish worship services.

But the start of Maimonides' rise to greatness in the realm of Jewish law was not without its difficulties. Indeed, at one time his works were ordered to be burned, and only with the passing of time were they highly honored as an authoritative code of

Jewish law. At one time Samuel ben Ali was a recognized scholar of the Talmud who became jealous of Maimonides' emerging prestige. Fearing that he would now be overshadowed, Samuel managed to involve Maimonides in a controversy over resurrection. As a result, Maimonides' views on the subject were more clearly delineated. In sum, he believed that the idea of the resurrection of humanity was not allegorical, but real. The resurrection of the body was against the rules of nature, explainable only as a miracle. He believed that those whose bodies were resurrected would live again for an extended life and then again suffer death. Thereafter, their souls but not their bodies would live on. Maimonides declared that humanity's last end is to know God.

Of Maimonides' many works, the greatest is *Guide for the Perplexed*, in which he showed how the teachings of Judaism harmonize with the great philosophical thinking, offering insights which reason alone cannot obtain. His first philosophical topic is God. In his work of exegesis he starts with an explanation of troublesome biblical terms relating to God, devoting the first forty-nine chapters to this task. He deals, for instance, with the phrase "God's image," in which humanity is said to have been formed. Some have argued that, if humans are made in God's image, it follows that God must have a physical body. Maimonides explains that the term *zelem* always refers to a spiritual quality, that is, an essence; therefore the image of God in people is their essence.

Maimonides also believed scholarship to be life's crowning achievement for humanity. He stated that scholars should be freed from work in order to pursue their growth in knowledge. His high ideals for scholars went beyond the mind, to include refinement of speech and even neatness of dress. He considered reason to be the chief of human faculties, and he violently opposed superstition and astrology. But his rationalism did not lead him to be a humanist. Rather, he taught that mankind was under divine providence.

Maimonides' intellectual contributions in the fields of religion, philosophy, and medicine have influenced Jewish and non-Jewish scholars alike. Without doubt he exerted a noticeable influence on Thomas Aquinas (recognized as the greatest philosopher-theologian of the Roman Catholic Church). He left his mark on physics and cosmology as well; and Albertus Magnus, Meister Eckart, Duns Scotus, Spinoza, and Moses Mendelssohn, all world-renowned thinkers, also bear the mark of his influence.

Before his time the philosophical study of Judaism was minor, but Maimonides made it the pursuit of a great many scholars. His attempts at reconciling Judaism with the teachings of Aristotle, brought reason and faith into harmony, and resulted in a renaissance of Talmudic study. As a codifier of the Law, Maimonides earned the name "the second Moses," and in the history of Jewish thought there is a great span arching over history from the one man to the other — prompting the well-known and highly complimentary phrase: "From Moses to Moses."

# Sir Thomas More

(1478-1535)

Very little is known of More's early childhood. His own memory of those first years was of a maid telling stories to him and his siblings. He loved animals, remembering with fascination the tales told him as a child about talking animals, and he never lost his attachment to Aesop's Fables and the animals with human voices. From early youth More exhibited the merriment of soul and a great sense of humour. His home life was happy and full of love, although his parents were stern in their moral teachings and their influence remained with him throughout his life. As an adult, he would often quote his father in his speeches and writings. More's father was a successful lawyer who became a judge of the Common Pleas Court in London and a justice of the King's Bench. At the age of eight his son was sent to one of the best schools in London, St. Anthony's, where Latin dominated the curriculum. More was a good scholar with a pronounced talent for creative writing, and was sufficiently precocious and original to write comedies in which he himself acted. Through the influence of his father, the youth caught the attention of the Archbishop of Canterbury, who brought him into his household. There More came in contact with a constant flow of visitors representing the best minds of the time. Because of the Archbishop, More studied Greek at Oxford, furthering his interest in all the classics represented in the Revival of Learning. Later More became a friend of Erasmus, the great Humanist, who had considerable influence upon him.

Although More outwardly exhibited a happy nature, he went through a great internal struggle as a young man. To please his father he studied law, against his own strong inclinations to enter the priesthood. (His father actually threatened to disown his son if he did not study law.) The Carthusian order had a special appeal for young More; in fact, while he pursued his legal studies and for a time after beginning practice, More lived for four years in the Carthusian Charter House in London. Thus, the two strongest elements influencing his later life were taking shape. His study of law, though against his wishes, would stand him in good stead during his later career as a government leader. His devotion to religion and to moral principles would give character to his activities as a world statesman.

As a young lawyer More was known to be scrupulously honest and meticulous with the cases he handled. He was always exceedingly well prepared before taking a case to court, and as a matter of character, he was said always to warn his clients that "they should not in a single detail turn from the truth." His success in the practice of law came rather quickly, so that he was soon involved in a great many of the famous cases of his time. More was a true scholar, retaining a strong interest in classical learning, and especially in Greek language and philosophy. Throughout his life he was an avid reader, roaming through the pages of literature, theology, philosophy, and history, and as a lecturer on these subjects, establishing a reputation as an eloquent and interesting speaker.

More's entrance into public life came with his appointment as under-sheriff of London and subsequent election to Parliament. Then followed, in rather rapid succession, the high offices of Privy Councillor, Master of Requests, Speaker of the House of Commons, Under-treasurer, Chancellor of the Duchy of Lancaster, and finally Lord High Chancellor, each step in his rise preparing him for the next. The position of under-sheriff was more like that of a city court judge than of the county law enforcement officer we know today. In this position More distinguished himself and gave the first indication of his great ability to speak extemporaneously. Thereafter he was to earn an ever-widening reputation for this particular talent. His emergence into truly national prominence came with his appointment as chancellor of the Duchy of Lancaster. This involved judiciary and administrative control over a large portion of northern England.

More's meteoric rise in public life came about, apart from his tremendous talents, through Henry VIII, who was eager to advance the cause of the Renaissance and sought to surround himself with outstanding men of letters. His attention was naturally called to Thomas More, foremost of such scholars in England at the time. The king appointed the young scholar to the Privy Council; then followed the long string of appointments to high offices. More was eventually elevated to knighthood, becoming a close friend and confidant of the king.

With his reputation at its peak, More made his greatest contribution to literature. *Utopia*, composed in Latin, guaranteed him a permanent place of prominence in literature and scholarship, taking its place among the classics as one of the most popular ever written. Evidence of the book's popularity is its translation into numerous languages, as well as the fact that 500 years after its creation it is still widely known and read. *Utopia* imagined the ideal state, but did so with a combination of insight and wit. An amazing number of the problems still plaguing society today were dealt with in this work, including marriage and divorce, unemployment, the rights of women, urban problems, crime, and others. The author left the realm of reality in imagining human nature completely without greed, selfishness, envy, or anger, but clearly defined the evils of his day and made them look ridiculous when paraded past self-deceived individuals.

More's concern for the emotional involvements of people is illustrated in his book, *Dialogue of Comfort Against Tribulation*. One of his works was written while he himself was undergoing great tribulation — *Dialogue Concerning Tyndale*, which was written in prison, prior to his execution. This was an attempt to expose forms of religious deceit; he argued both sides of the Tyndale controversy and spoke out vigorously against relics, as well as what many supposed to be miracles in those days. He sought to expose the fallacy of pilgrimages. Thus, More can be thought of as the middle man, even the reconciler of Roman Catholic-Protestant schisms. He lived just prior to the separation of the two great Christian divisions. And, while a loyal supporter of the Pope, he yet was a champion of "basic religion." Though he died before the great split in Christendom, More could see it coming and he fought to prevent it. He urged a return to the Bible, and to a study of the Church Fathers and to Greek. In these current years of emphasis on ecumenism, he can well serve as a model for reconciliation.

The divorces of Henry VIII were to bring many upheavals in church and society. In the life of Thomas More they were to be cataclysmic. He had risen to power and authority in govern-ment until he occupied the high post of Lord Chancellor. There he demonstrated his religious loyalties by ordering monastic re-forms and in supporting the Roman Church against heresy. But when Henry VIII divorced Catherine to marry Anne Boleyn, More resigned his post. His unwavering fidelity to his church caused his death, for he refused to take an oath acknowledging the king, who had now made himself head of the Church of England, as supreme in matters of religion. More's last words were a tribute to the place of religion in his life, and to his personal faith as the directing force in that life, when he said "I die in and for the faith of the Catholic Church; the King's loyal servant, but God's first."

While his father harbored great ambitions for him in every way, Thomas had never been interested in gaining wealth, nor in social climbing. He got along well with people, but found his greatest joy in those social contacts where he could take part in intellectual conversations. He established a close relationship with Erasmus, a friendship which helped to inspire his permanent in-terest in the classics and the Renaissance. These two men carried on a constant correspondence throughout their lives, and Eras-mus paid the highest tribute to his friend, apparently appreciat-ing highly his humor, his mind, and the great enjoyment of his company. But it was only through the strong urging of Erasmus that More was induced to publish some of his writings. Erasmus once penned this high compliment, "What has nature ever creat-ed more gentle, more sweet, more happy, than the genius of Tho-mas More?" and even dedicated to More his famous work, *In Praise of Folly*. For several years Erasmus lived with More and his family in the home they called "The Barge."

When More first entered Parliament he quickly distinguished himself as a man of bold convictions, ably expressed. But in spite of his rapid rise and recognition as a man of letters, student of the law, and member of Parliament, it was religion and theology which dominated More's life. It seems astonishing that the man so well known in public life voluntarily adopted the daily regi-men followed by the Franciscan order of monks; this even includ-ed the rigors of wearing a hair shirt, which he did all his life, as well as fasting, keeping daily prayer vigils, and engaging in meditation. He would sleep on boards and rise at two a.m. for prayer. These practices did not, however, preclude him from marrying twice, raising a family, and giving much time to the education and development of his children. Though he became famous as a nation's political leader, More's religious devotion continued to be an outstanding characteristic throughout his life. When in prison, the day before he was executed, he sent his hair shirt home to his wife.

Shocked at the news of his dear friend's beheading, Erasmus wrote that More was one "whose soul was more pure than any snow, whose genius was such that England never had, and never again will have, the like."

# Blaise Pascal

(1623-1662)

Here is a man whose tremendous contribution to knowledge and to religion may well be underestimated. A scientist of the first rank, scientists honor him as the founder of hydrodynamics. He is applauded also as one of the greatest physicists of all time, and as the developer of the theory of mathematical probability. In addition to all of this, Pascal has been recorded in history for his important theory of conic sections, and for his investigations of gravity and vacuum. Such an array of talent with its attendant honors would seem to suffice for one individual. But there is much more to his story. Completely apart from the field of science, Pascal has established a lasting reputation in such diverse fields as literature and psychology. In the former, one can gain insight into his preeminent contribution by realizing that he is credited with creating the modern French style of writing. Finally, religion was so strong a factor in his life that he excelled there, too, coming to be known as well in the fields of religion and philosophy as he was in science.

Pascal was born in Clermont, a French village in the province of Ferrand, on June 17, 1623. His mother died when he was only three, and when he was a lad of eight, his father moved to Paris in order to devote himself to the education of his son — who was already displaying the remarkable precociousness that would mark his entire life. While still a boy, Pascal showed such aptitude for mathematics that he is claimed to have been able, on his own, to work out the first thirty-two propositions of the first book of Euclid. To the average reader this may not mean much but such a feat is one attained by only the brightest among mature geometricians. Pascal was only sixteen when he authored a treatise on conic sections which so impressed Leibnitz that the famous mathematician urged its immediate publication, praising its originality and importance. But proof of his inventive genius and of its practical applications also came early in his career. For example, during a period of his youth when his father was a tax collector, young Pascal enjoyed helping him, but found that long and tedious cal-culations were often necessary in the work. Deciding to do some-thing about it, he created, at the age of twenty, a machine which automaticallly worked out the troublesome, arithmetical problems.

Again, his interest was directed to a study of vacuum, where his discoveries became the authoritative norm in that field. So great was his contribution to this and related fields that encyclopedias have dated the advent of modern physics from the experiments and conclusions of Pascal made in 1648 when he was only twenty-five years of age.

Sometimes the appearance of genius is unexplainable. In other cases some contributing causes can be detected. In the early bloom-ing of Pascal, one definite influence was the interest which his father took in him as a child. The elder Pascal was a cultured man of the world with a love of learning. He had confidence that he alone was the best teacher for his offspring, and insisted that his son study languages, including Latin and Greek, and that he also study literature as well as mathematics. It was he who instilled in his son a dedication to originality, a questioning spirit which took nothing for granted, and a revulsion for prejudice. Together, father and son studied the greatest thinkers and philosophers, resulting in a precocious young mind which was constantly stretched and challenged to its limits.

But while Pascal's mind was usually active, his bodily health was precarious. At the age of eighteen his physical condition was frail and he said that from that time onward he "did not spend one day without pain." All the more remarkable was it, there-fore, that he could be so productive. Fortunately his contributions did come early, for he died at the age of thirty-nine. Neverthe-less, Pascal left behind a strong and enduring influence on the world — and has been fittingly described as "a man among the heroes of mankind."

It was because he had become dissatisfied with abstract science that Pascal was led to study humankind and the spiritual realm. Instantly, he became a serious seeker after "truth," bringing a fine sense of balance into his religious thinking which was to charac-terize his writings in this field. For instance, while refusing to acknowledge human reason as the great source of truth, Pascal nevertheless defended the strengths and capability of the human mind. He believed that God permitted humanity to come to a knowledge of profound religious truths by means of reason, but that the real comprehension came from rising above human reason to divine grace. He comprehended truth to be the expression of God's will, and a means by which one might come to know and love God. Pascal did not believe that people could or should be converted by force, but he believed that individuals should show the proper initiative in the fields of religion and morality. Two of his greatest literary works are *Letress Provinciales*, and *Pensees*. The first could be considered a defense of the faith; the second deals psychologically and theologically with the fundamental problems of human existence. Both books have had a significent influence on human thought.

When he was about twenty-three, Pascal had a religious experience which he called an "ecstasy," and which he recorded in his personal papers. This spiritual illumination raised him above the interests which had absorbed him up to that time, and as a result, a great change took place in him. Now his previous interests were judged to be materials for heavenly contemplation; this was the turning point whereby a genius in science became a leader in religious thought. While he continued to honor human reason, he elevated inspiration as a new-found, higher power. Now he came to give credit for originality not to the human heart, but to God acting on the human spirit.

As his interest in religion deepened, Pascal even became interested in the cloistered life. While he did not become a member of a convent he was an adherent of the Port Royal monastic recluses in Paris. He was thirty-two when he moved in among these brethren. Occasionally, he would leave the order to live for a time in the city, but would then return. It was here that a well-known event in his life took place. On display in the convent was a thorn said to be from the crown of thorns that was placed on the head of Christ. Now Pascal had a niece, Marguerite Perier, who was then ten years old and who suffered from an ulcer on her eye. She came to the convent and placed the thorn on her eye, praying for a cure. When the cure materialized, Pascal was so impressed that, when creating a personal emblem, he included in it an eye, surrounded by a crown of thorns, and the motto *Scio cui credidi*, I know whom I have believed."

Pascal saw humanity as an impotent creature, limited in thought, subjected to misery. Yet he was not pessimistic in his concept. For he conceived that we humans are not left to ourselves in our state of weakness and despair, that God is near, and that faith is the bridge by which one reaches God. Thus, while Pascal believed that there are limits to human reason, he also believed that within those limits human reason is trustworthy; but more importantly, and this is a key thought of his, "there are reasons which transcend human reason."

Emphasizing his belief that God is revealed in the person of Jesus Christ, and not by human reason, Pascal wrote, "The God of the Christians is not a God who is simply the theory of geometric truths. This is the God of the pagan. He is not a God who crowns with blessings those who serve Him. This is the God of the Jews. The God of the Christians is a God of love and consecration, a God who unites Himself with the ground of their being and fills them with humility, joy, confidence and love. He makes the soul feel that its peace lies wholly in Him, and that it has no joy save to love Him. To know God after this fashion one must know first one's own misery and worthlessness and the need of a mediator in order to approach God, and be united with Him. The knowledge of God without the recognition of our misery engenders pride. The recognition of our misery without Jesus Christ produces despair. But the knowledge of Christ frees us alike from pride and despair because here we find conjoined God and our misery and the only way in which it can be repaired."

In Pascal's day there arose a critic within the Roman Catholic Church by the name of Cornelius Jansen. He was to give rise to a movement known as Jansenism, which in turn would produce a sect within Roman Catholicism that called itself The Jansenist Catholic Church, persisting through coming generations, though never as a strong movement. Jansen, an Augustinian, was a devout Catholic and Bishop of Ypres. But he strongly opposed the Jesuit Order within his church because of their semi-Pelagian interpretations of sin and grace. He did not believe that one should do good works in the belief that they could earn salvation, an impossible task, but that one should do good works out of gratitude and love for the God who freely gives salvation and grace to the unworthy sinner. His views were adopted by the nunnery of Port

Royal, thus engulfing Pascal in the rising protests. Pascal has been described as a Calvinist Catholic because of his stress on rigorous morals and for his acceptance of the doctrine of predestination. In propounding his views, Pascal wrote *Les Provinciales*, which defended the Jansenists and attacked the philosophy and theology of the Jesuits. The Pope opposed his writings and the King of France followed suit. But even though opposed by such powerful forces, Pascal persisted in his views.

Later Pascal produced the volume, *The Pensees* (thoughts), in which he turned from attacking the Jesuits within the church to attacking the atheists outside it. Concerned about the influence of the non-Christian free-thinkers who were becoming prominent, his aim was to bring back to the faith those whom these free-thinkers had influenced. The work was not published until 1669, seven years after his death, but his publications, particularly *The Pensees*, were to establish Pascal as one of the greatest of religious thinkers, whose influence would be considerable in shaping the thoughts of intellectual leaders for centuries to come.

Thus, a man who for all time is enshrined within the pages of history as an outstanding scientist and man of literature, became equally known for his lasting contribution to philosophers and theologians of coming generations.

# Benedictus De Spinoza
(Baruch)

### (1632-1677)

Spinoza was born of Jewish parents in Spain, from which country the family was exiled to Portugal while the boy was still young. He was forced to undergo the pain of resettlement a second time when the family was again exiled, finally finding his permanent home in Holland. Spinoza's father was a successful merchant, sufficiently faithful to his religion to want his son to become a rabbi. As a result, young Spinoza studied the Hebrew Bible, the Talmud, and Jewish literature of an earlier day. But his mind was stretched also by the study of Latin, natural sciences, and great philosophers, especially Hobbes and Descartes; the final result was that, enamored of philosophy, he chose that field over the rabbinate. He was to gain a world-wide and lasting fame as a philosopher who made a significant contribution to theology as well. Ultimately the philosopher broke with orthodox Judaism, but retained profound religious convictions throughout his life, and the nature of God was one of his chief emphases. His interest lay in learning the truth and expanding it, so he can accurately be termed an investigative philosopher. But though he avidly studied the great philosophers, he thoroughly examined the Bible as well as the Talmud, for his great aim was to reveal the mystery of God and the meaning of human life.

While we think of Spinoza as a man who lived with deep thoughts, we need to remember that he was also a man of practical experience who could earn a living for himself in the marketplace. He learned the art of making lenses and ground them with sufficient perfection to be able to support himself from this source of income. Throughout his life, Spinoza studiously avoided any entanglements that would prevent him from speaking the truth as he saw it. He turned down offers of money and position in order not to be compromised in any way, and in place of mansions he chose a one-room existence. At the age of 24 he was excommunicated by the orthodox synagogue for his heterodox ideas, which he firmly believed to be the truth and which, therefore, he could not alter. His sister sought to take advantage of his excommunication by having his inclusion in his parent's will voided, but he went to court and won the case. He then, however, promptly turned over his portion to the sister who had sought it. Spinoza was so much the philosopher, thinker, and scholar that he completely disdained material wealth, intentionally living a plain existence, and rejecting all efforts of friends to increase his financial well-being. He refused to accept sizeable gifts, including the grant of a large estate from a friend who wished to will him his fortune, though he did accept a bequest from another friend when the annuity was lowered from $250 to $150. He turned down the offer of a pension from King Louis XIV, both because of his attitude toward wealth and because of unacceptable provisions attached to the pension.

Spinoza has been given the unusual and highly complimentary title, "the God-intoxicated philosopher." This spiritual emphasis became clear in Spinoza's first published book. Dealing with theology, not philosophy, it was entitled: *A Treatise on Religion,* and underscored his break with the orthodox branch of his Jewish faith. He withdrew his support of the harsh and stern God of wrath, and subscribed to a God of mercy, a view which would make him more tolerant of Christianity. Spinoza accepted Jesus as the voice of God incarnate, as the way of life, and held that the dogmas of Christianity should be judged, in the final analysis, in terms of their effectiveness in stirring the heart to piety. Spinoza was a man of personal piety, and of a benevolent spirit, described as possessing a loving personality; and a man of innocence who loved the common people and disclaimed the splendor of kings and statesmen. In attacking the Bible, Spinoza directed his fire at portions of the Old Testament, due to his acceptance of the principle of separation of church and state; for the Old Testament supported the idea of a politico-religious community, while the New Testament proclaimed the salvation of individuals. He was, in short, a man who "walked humbly with his God."

In his penetrating thoughts, Spinoza contemplated the three areas that cover all existence: Humankind; the world, or universe in which we live; and the God who created it all. As for the universe, his main thoughts, put in simplest form, stated that (1) it is eternal, complete, everlasting; (2) it is infinite, having no end in space; (3) the world is but a tiny speck in the vastness of the universe, and there are other universes beyond our own.

As for humankind, Spinoza believed that we came into being as the creation of God, but that God is a part of us, and the eternal "I am" of whom all existence is a part. Though he is within us, he is too great for our finite minds to comprehend more than a fraction of him. He is the intelligence that directs all things; he is an artist and the universe is his canvas; he is energy. Because of God, the Creator, mankind is in a constant state of development, and beyond our earthly existence is a far greater realm of growth, a constant elevation to ever higher degrees of existence. As an artist, God is in every individual, no matter what his condition or situation, painting the great tapestry of time and space. Therefore, every individual is important.

Spinoza stressed love as the supreme emotion, with power to transform life and human situations. He saw it as the eternal element in humankind which lives on after the body dies. It is the nature of God in us, the imprint of the maker upon the created. Spinoza declared that "the love of man to God and the love of man to man are one and the same." He believed that religion consists of love more than doctrine.

It was after Spinoza had moved to Voorburg, near the Hague, that he published, in 1670, the celebrated *Tractus Theologica-Politicus*. In its preface he wrote, "I show that the Word of God has not been revealed as a certain number of books, but was displayed to the prophets as a simple idea of the divine mind, namely obedience to God in singleness of heart, and in the practice of justice and charity; and I further point out that this doctrine is set forth in Scripture in accordance with the opinion and understanding of those among whom the apostles and prophets preached, to the end that men might receive it willingly, and with their whole heart."

In this work, Spinoza pleads, in logical fashion, for freedom of thought and speech. A large part of the publication is devoted to his investigation of the sacred Scriptures, through which he encouraged modern biblical criticism. Spinoza described the Bible as being not a source for man's searching for philosophical or scientific truth, but for moral guidance alone, and declared that the scriptures are "imaginational" rather than rational, that their purpose is to win loyalty to moral laws and to the advancement of justice and charity. He saw the Bible as "necessary for salvation among men who do not possess high intellectual gifts — namely, the majority of men" but felt it should in no way limit the free exercise of the human intellect in searching for truth.

Spinoza's chief work is entitled *Ethics*, in which he sets forth his belief that a person's search for God influences personal behaviour, that philosophical thought leads to the improvement of the thinker. He stated that reason and science could end in bringing the same influence on human behaviour as did religious traditions. When one studies nature, he declared, one is studying God, and it is important for one to attain union with the whole of nature. Such study and resultant knowledge brings both moral evaluation and unceasing joy.

Spinoza criticized the Bible in its entirety, New Testament as well as Old, but he did so in the spirit of scholarly research rather than that of an iconoclast. He was really in the company of modern biblical higher criticism, but his criticisms made him enemies among both Jews and Christians, and he himself was criticized in turn. It was not until long after his death that he was given his greatest honors and recognition. In his lifetime, he did, however, receive acclaim, and some honors which he could not decline even though he shrank from publicity. He was recognized for his high qualities of thought and life by many leaders of his day, but remained a man of humble spirit. When offered the chair of philosophy at the prestigious Heidelberg University, Spinoza declined the appointment, thinking it would be apt to restrict his freedom of thought and honesty of declarations. It was not until after his death that he came into full recognition as one of the greatest philosophers of all time. This praise was encouraged by the acclaim given him a century later by the German philosopher, Johann Herder and the author-scientist Johann Goethe, both of whom became known as Spinozists. But Joseph Ernest Renan paid a sterling tribute to Spinoza's spiritual dimension when speaking at the dedication of a statue of Spinoza at the Hague in 1882, he said, "Here came perhaps the truest vision ever had of God."

# William Penn

(1644-1718)

William Penn's name will always be kept alive in America because of the great American state which bears his name, but this unusual honor was one which he neither sought nor desired. He tried to eliminate his name and call the state Sylvania rather than Pennsylvania, and it was only the insistence on the part of a king who admired him that caused his name to be thus forever honored.

William Penn was outstanding as a pioneer in the early development of the United States, dreaming great dreams and carrying them to fulfilment. He was, as well, a capable statesman and governor, and most certainly a man of religious leadership and devotion.

His father was a naval officer, rising to the rank of Admiral, and led the expedition which won Jamaica from the Spaniards, making it the ninth British Colony in the Caribbean West Indies. Later he was knighted and served in the House of Commons. Penn's parents greatly enjoyed social life, delighting in holiday parties, attending the theater, and absorbing themselves in the lighter side of life. It was partly in reaction to what he saw as frivolous society that Penn began to search for life's deeper, spiritual meanings.

William early became a lover of freedom, which he was to champion so strongly in later life. As a student at Oxford he was expelled because he engaged in a student demonstration against required chapel attendance. But he made it clear that his opposition was not to religious teaching but rather to the coercion of forced attendance. At the same time, Penn's personal life was one of strict observance of his religious beliefs. Once, when faced with a charge of deceitfulness or falsehood in his personal life, he was able to face his detractors with this statement, "I make this bold challenge to all men . . . justly to accuse me with ever having seen me drunk, heard me swear, utter a curse, or speak one obscene word — much less that I make it a practice."

Penn played a significant part in the early development of the future United States, and he did so from strong religious convictions. He first helped George Fox to secure for Quakers, through purchase, West Jersey in 1674 and East Jersey in 1681. Speaking of the documents drawn up by Quakers on this territory, Penn wrote, "There we lay a foundation for after-ages to understand their liberty as men and Christians, that they may not be trampled in bondage." When then he secured Pennsylvania from the Crown he wrote of that territory, "My God that has given it me through many difficulties, will, I believe, bless and make it the seed of a nation . . . I have so obtained it and desire to keep it, that I may not be unworthy of His love; but do that which may answer His kind providence and serve His Truth and people." The laws of the first Assembly provided for the observance of Sunday as a day of rest, "for the ease of the Creation," and for the opportunity for worship, and it is quite clear that Penn was as definitely moved by religious purposes in the founding of Pennsylvania as were the Puritans in founding Massachusetts.

There was this difference, however; the Puritan government was based on a theocracy, while Penn's was founded as a democracy. There was this further difference, that while the Puritans sought to establish a righteous state by excluding any who could not conform to their religious beliefs, Penn offered to include individuals who differed, for he believed that all people should follow the dictates of their own consciences. In so doing he declared, "We must give the liberty we ask. We cannot be false to our principles . . . I abhor two principles in religion and pity them that own them; the first is obedience to authority without conviction; and the other is destroying them that differ from me for God's sake." However he did place certain limits on the extension of freedom to all by restricting both the right to hold public office and to vote to "such as profess faith in Jesus Christ." Penn placed great trust in the character which people exhibited. He wrote, "Governments rather depend upon men more than men upon governments. Let men be good, and the government cannot be bad . . . But if men be bad, let the government be ever so good, they will endeavor to warp and spoil it to their turn."

Penn was noted for his fairness and his insistence upon proper treatment of one's neighbor. This was emphasized in his dealings with the Indians, as he strongly opposed the ill-treatment given them by many Americans. His treaty with the Indians in November, 1682, was described by the cynical Voltaire as "the only treaty ever made without an oath, and the only treaty never broken." It has been said that Penn was the main reason it was never broken, and he was described as a man who would rather go to prison than break his word.

Though he accomplished much that made him well-known on both sides of the Atlantic Ocean, Penn's religion was the dominant factor in his life. His aim in establishing his settlement in the New World was to create a Christian state on a Quaker model. His most important book bears the title, of religious significance, *No Cross, No Crown*.

Penn's life was not always peaceful, for he was involved in many conflicts and was imprisoned several times, mostly because of his religious convictions. He held to them steadfastly, and on such grounds refused to remove his hat in the presence of the King. But more will be said of his trials later.

Penn's faith was based upon his belief in the interrelatedness of God and society, and believed that faith was a practical matter. His contribution to the Quakers as a strong and distinguishable religious force was significant, for he provided both a theological and political dynamic, without which the movement probably would not have survived. Through him it emerged from the cloud of a questionable future into a religious force which has made a strong Christian impression.

The accomplishments of this man were enormous. The true measure of his attainments can best be grasped when one considers the tremendous obstacles he had to overcome. Out of the wilderness with all its hardships and deprivations, Penn brought forth in Pennsylvania an orderly society and a very respectable colony. The territory he had been granted was huge, part of the uncultured frontier, populated with "savages" and a few frontiersmen. But he plunged into the task of creating a modern settlement out of the vast wilderness. Penn's first problem was the Indians. To the amazement of many, he succeeded in establishing good relations with them, forming treaties which were respected by both parties. The native Americans came to know Penn as a man who could be trusted, in stark contrast to the dishonesty of many other white men of that time, and paid the Indians for additional land, rather than attempting to gain it by unfair means. The office of

Governor included numerous and exhausting requirements, but Penn filled it with tact, efficiency and distinction. He developed the plans for the city of Philadelphia, laying out its streets and its four great squares, set aside for parkland which exists today. He arranged for the sale of lands to immigrants, oversaw the necessary surveying, and made sure that purchase prices were just. In adddition he set up a judicial system of courts, laid out roads, built a governor's mansion, and attended meetings of the Quakers as a religious man and of the Assembly as a statesman.

Travel in those days was nearly impossible, and his many trips, riding on horseback in all kinds of weather, must have been hard on his health, but because he wanted the best inhabitants possible in his territory, Penn spent much time in portraying the benefits of the land to people in England, encouraging industrious farmers and skilled artisans to immigrate to his land. Penn personally financed a considerable portion of the cost of developing his colony in its infancy, and he was forced to keep in constant contact with those around the throne in England in order to defend his enterprise from those who sought to take the land from him.

Throughout his lifetime Penn was imprisoned several times because of the work of his enemies. They succeeded at times in having him jailed for his preaching, for his Quaker faith, or for his writings, but the help of influential friends in high places gained him his release.

There can be no question that Penn was a man of high character. Although, through his constant contacts with the royal courts of his day, he was forced into the company of many who were frivolous and even immoral, his association with such monarchs and those who surrounded them did not lead Penn to copy their behavior. He was dedicated to the biblical injunction to "keep oneself unspotted from the world." Once, in telling his daughter that she should not be worldly, he defined worldliness as anything that cools one's affection for Christ. Penn revealed the source of his devotion to high morals and good character in his Journal. There he tells how he came as a young man to know a young Quaker preacher named Thomas Loe. Penn wrote, "It was in this way that God in His everlasting goodness guided my feet in the flower of my youth when I was about twenty years of age. He visited me with a certain sound and testimony of His eternal Word through a Quaker named Thomas Loe." The particular sermon of Loe's which made a lasting impression on Penn was based on 1 John 5:5 which reads, "This is the victory which overcometh the world, even our faith." Penn took this text as his personal inspiration and thereafter stressed faith in God to the point of letting it shape his life. His Journals attest to the fact that Penn sensed the nearness of God in his life and was confident that the Lord had sustained him through all of his trials.

Penn's last years, unfortunately, were filled with so much disappointnment and trouble that his faith was sorely tested. His son, William, turned out to be a real disappointment, keeping the wrong company, becoming an alcoholic, and accumulating considerable debt. After his father helped him to meet his obligations, young William continued to be a spendthrift and went into bankruptcy a second time. He further hurt his father by rejecting his religious faith.

In addition to this, Penn, himself an honest man, put too much trust in others. He put Philip Ford, for instance, in charge of his business affairs, since he himself was involved in many other responsibilities and had to travel much, including trips back and forth across the Atlantic Ocean. Ford betrayed Penn's trust, falsifying the financial records and cheating his benefactor out of a considerable sum. Penn came close to losing all his vast holdings in Pennsylvania, and to make matters worse, after Ford's death, his widow took Penn to court on false charges, based on her former husband's conniving. When Penn appealed to his friends in America for some assistance, they turned their backs on him en masse, even though they owed their own pleasant circumstances to him.

Finally, in 1712, Penn suffered the first of three paralytic strokes. Though he recovered to the point of becoming ambulatory again, his mind was weakened, and for the next few years until his death, Penn withdrew from public life into the family circle, where his daughter and her children were a great source of comfort to him.

History has enhanced the name of Penn, as the territory he developed has become one of the great states in the Union. He endured almost overwhelming hardships, in the rigors of frontier living, in overcoming the obstacles in the way of fulfilling his dreams, and in the betrayal of those whom he had helped and

trusted. But, witnessing the great heritage he left behind, both religiously and politically, in spite of all his difficulties, it is good
to see that his mighty acts have rendered his reputation forever
secure in the name of the great State of Pennsylvania.

# Johann Sebastian Bach

(1685-1750)

One must beware of an accolade when describing someone as "the greatest." In all fields of human endeavor there have been many who have reached the pinnacle of success, and there is always room for argument as to which is foremost. But when it comes to music, J. S. Bach appears to boast the greatest number of experts willing to put him in first place. Tributes to him include these statements:, "He was perhaps the greatest musician who ever lived; and the most influential," "One of the greatest musical geniuses of all time," "No one has ever had so much influence on music and musicians world wide as J. S. Bach," and "Bach produced some of the most sublime music in the history of the Church." Similar praise is heaped upon his B Minor Mass, which has been called "the greatest musical composition in the world." On the 300th anniversary of his birth, when most once-famous men lie forgotten in their graves, Bach was selected for honor and recognition by great city symphonies, hailed on television and other media, and his music was selected for presentation in special recitals by outstanding musicians worldwide. *Newsweek Magazine* declared that Bach is "not a bygone figure dimly perceived, but a living presence to whom almost everything in music past and present is somehow indebted."

J. S. Bach came from a family with a long heritage of musical talent and genius. Indeed, the researcher must keep in mind the initials of this great man in order not to be confused by the number of Bachs within the same family, all musicians, some quite distinguished. His father, his brother, some of his children, all bearing the same family name, gave their lives to music. It was a closely knit family, one that regularly gathered from a wide territory to enjoy a family reunion, and at such times, music was the principal entertainment. It has been reported that the first known member of the family in Germany, a man named Veit Bach, waiting for his wheat to be ground, thoroughly enjoyed playing his guitar in the midst of the noise and confusion from the grinding wheels of the mill. With such a cultural heritage, it is not surprising that J. S. Bach would come forth to thrill the world with his music. Yet, wide-spread recognition was late in coming, for during his lifetime Bach's fame was limited to his native Germany. Only after his death was Bach given the preeminence he can claim today. In fact, it was not until a number of decades after his death that he was widely acclaimed as one of the three immortal "B's" of the musical world: Bach, Beethoven and Brahms.

J. S. Bach was born in Eisenach, East Germany on March the first, 1685. This territory is rich in the tradition of Martin Luther, and the influence of the Reformer was strong in Bach's life. He lived near the Wartburg Castle where Luther had translated the New Testament, and, when he attended Latin School in Eisenach at the age of eight he was attending the same school where Luther had once enrolled. A Luther translation of the Bible was his prized possession, which he re-read countless times, and so great was the Reformer's influence on Bach that a German historian once declared that after three centuries the only German who really understood Luther was Bach.

Bach's mother had three children who lived, of whom he was the youngest. She died when he was only nine years old and his father passed away less than a year later. Bach then went to live with an older brother, Johann Cristoff Bach, but it is believed that before he died his father began giving young Johann lessons on the violin. The youth apparently had a good voice, too, for he not only sang in the school choir and the choir of St. George's Church, but was able partially to support himself with his voice. His brother initiated his lifelong display of musical talent by teaching him to play the clavichord and the harpsichord, and he played other instruments as well, including the flute, trumpet and oboe.

But it was when he learned to play the organ that Bach discovered his real love in the realm of music. Thereafter, he was to carve out a national reputation during his own lifetime as an organist. From the age of eighteen onward he served a succession of positions as church organist, and along the way held the position of court organist for the Duke of Saxe-Weimar. It was while he was at Weimar that Bach attained a preeminent reputation as an unusually gifted organist. In large part this was due to the fact that he was permitted to travel at rather frequent intervals. On these journeys he played at various courts and churches, where he won the acclaim of many audiences and became known as Germany's organ virtuoso. But his spreading fame throughout Germany was as an organist rather than a composer. It seems surprising that his works were not popular in his own time, but this was due to the fact that he was ahead of his time. His contemporaries considered his composition to be dry and old-fashioned, not even equal in appeal to the compositions of his sons. It was not until the talented Felix Mendelssohn revived Bach's *Passion According to St. Matthew*, seventy-nine years after the composer's death, that Bach's position in the musical world was finally established for all time. Thereafter he came into his own as a composer as well as an organist, and when his music was finally discovered by famous musicians, due to the efforts of Mendelssohn, they eagerly turned to playing his masterpieces. But more will be said later of Mendelssohn's part in this "discovery" of Bach the composer. In his own day Bach enjoyed a prominent position as a judge of organs, and as a skilled expert in the construction of such instruments. As such, he did considerable travelling throughout Germany, both to counsel churches installing organs and to play at the first formal concert of the new instruments. He is recognized as the pioneer of the modern system of tuning keyboard instruments.

Bach's first wife, a cousin, died after thirteen years of marriage. Of their seven children, four were living at the time of their mother's death. Eighteen months later he remarried and this wife, Anna Wilcken, bore him ten more children.

Bach was a devout Lutheran who made a singular contribution to his church's musical repertoire. His interest in theology led him to read widely in that field, and he accumulated a fine theological library, including two complete sets of Luther's works. He was deeply influenced by the Lutheran preaching of his day, which he heard on so many occasions when he played for church services. He really lived out his life work as a deeply religious man, one who believed that all of life was God-related. His personal Bible has been recovered and the fact that it shows much wear and contains many personal markings and annotations is proof that he was an ardent Bible reader and student. Bach was convinced that this life is followed by eternity for those who accept Christ into their lives, and there is a definite Christian foundation to all of Bach's works. He was actually a preacher of the Gospel, one who presented the inspiration of the Scriptures, but his preaching took the form of musical composition. The famous Swedish Archbishop, Soderblom, called Bach the "fifth evangelist" because of his inspired musical settings for the Sunday Bible readings. He has been praised as being next in importance to Martin Luther himself in shaping worship in Lutheran congregations. Bach felt inspired to create the "music of eternity," as he emphasized the spiritual in his creations.

When he left the position in Weimar to go Leipzig it was with a reduction in salary, but Bach went gladly because, he said, at Saint Thomas School in Leipzig he could "lead a congregation toward Christ." He could say this because every week for four years he composed a cantata which expressed musically the theme and words of the Sunday Bible lessons. These compositions were the principal music in the service, based on the designated scriptural lessons for the day, with the aim of emphasizing those lessons and making the congregation receptive to them. A Bach concerto therefore has been likened to a musical sermon. His music portrayed his strong faith in God, his deep love of Christ, and his acceptance of death as the portal to eternal life. He did not need large choirs to make his music impressive; rather he used choral groups of about a dozen singers. He composed a great many hymns for the Lutheran Church, among them the well-known and beloved *Jesu, Joy of Man's Desiring*. So devoutly religious was Bach, and so willing to declare openly his faith in Christ and his love of God, that he initialed his compositions with the three letters "INS" representing the Latin words meaning "in the name of Jesus." At other times Bach began his score with the letters "JJ," for the Latin phrase *Jesu Juva*, meaning "Jesus help," and then ended his composition with the letters "SDG" for the Latin *Sola Deo Gloria*, meaning "to God alone be the glory."

It is said that his older brother Chris, with whom he went to live after the death of his parents, was responsible for this religious dedication, for he impressed his younger brother with the challenge to create music not just for enjoyment or entertainment, but as a tribute to God. A further insight into his deeply religious character is gained from his application for the position of organist at Leipzig. Bach wrote that if hired, among other things, he would set his students "a shining example of an honest, retiring manner of life." Furthermore, he wrote that his music would "be of such a nature as not to make an operatic impression, but rather incite the listeners to devotion." He copied Luther's emphasis on love for one's neighbor by writing in the introduction to his organ teaching book: "for my neighbor's greater skill."

Though it took some decades for Bach to acquire universal recognition as a true musical genius, his influence has since been tremendous. To name those great musicians whom he strongly influenced is like reciting the "Who's Who" of the musical world. His influence was felt by such great composers as Mozart, Haydn, Beethoven, Liszt, Brahms, Gounod, Wagner and Mendelssohn.

Though his enduring works are far and away too numerous to mention in this short biography, one feels compelled to credit the great composer with such compositions as *The Magnificat, The St. Matthew Passion, The B Minor Mass, The Brandenburg Concertos, The Well Tempered Clavichord, and St. John's Passion.* The range of his musical works is rather amazing. Some were for the voice, some for various instruments. At times he composed church music, at other times music for the ballroom, and again for the concert hall. He gladdened hosts of people by his compositions for weddings, coronations, baptisms, birthdays, and offered special consolation at funerals. There was one area of musical composition however, which he missed, for he wrote no operas. On the other hand, his influence reached beyond the field of music, for the great philosopher, Hegel, was one of his ardent boosters. Albert Schweitzer wrote of Bach: "Any room becomes a church in which his sacred works are performed and listened to with devotion." But one is truly amazed to read the statement by Nietsche, so well known as a non-believer, "One who has completely forgotten Christianity hears it here as Gospel." He was moved to make this statement after hearing the *St. Matthew Passion* in 1870.

Bach finished his life by living and serving at St. Thomas Church in Leipzig, until failing health forced his retirement. He became nearly blind at age 64, two years before his death following a stroke. The last year of his life was lived amid a happy family situation, and unable to see, he yet continued his productivity by dictating musical compositions, mostly hymns, to two of his young students. Bach died in Leipzig on July 28, 1750, unaware that future generations around the world would proclaim this man who never crossed the boundaries of his own nation to be one of the world's greatest musicians of all time. It must have been gratifying to him to know that he was leaving behind him sons who would carry on the musical tradition of the Bach family.

Bach's works are still being discovered and played today. But the original effort that brought back to the world the inspiration of the great composer was due to two men. One must remember that Bach died as a distinguished organist, but one whose compositions were not generally known or appreciated. He would probably not even be remembered today were it not for Karl Friedrich Zelter and one of his pupils, Felix Mendellssohn, who early in life was recognized as a musical genius. Zelter was a scholarly musician who somehow was acquainted with the music of the then almost forgotten Bach. Willing to go against the judgment of the day, which considered Bach music to be archaic, Zelter taught it to his pupils, one of whom was Mendelssohn. The boy, Felix, was consumed with the desire to play Bach's works and after Mendelssohn, as a very young man, had achieved great distinction, he persuaded Zelter, director of the Berlin Singing Academy to loan 158 singers for the chorus and the use of the impressive hall of the Academy for rehearsal and presentation of the *St. Matthew Passion*. In spite of discouraging words, the youthful Felix worked diligently to bring the production to perfection. Word spread that something unusual was being prepared for music lovers, and on the night of the performance, the hall was filled to overflowing and the crowd was rapturous in its praise. Bach had been rediscovered and his name given to eternity. It is a beautiful paradox that a young Jewish musician, Felix Mendelssohn, was the means of bringing to light the now famous music which is the delight and inspiration of all music lovers, but especially those of the Christian world.

# Sir Edmund Burke

(1730-1797)

Edmund Burke was a great statesman who, at the same time, was one of the best examples of lofty and unreproachable character. In the field of statesmanship he is compared to none other than Cicero, but along with that reputation, his character shines forth as one who is religious, conscientious and upright. He is a veritable symbol of political morality, a vigorous opponent of government corruption in any form. There may be differences of opinion concerning his political views, but there is unanimous respect for Edmund Burke's character. His political career is noteworthy for producing a great many outstanding reforms, emanating from his sense of moral justice, and Burke is frequently quoted by the most outstanding of his followers in the legislative halls on three continents as a model of governmental leadership. He has been called the most remarkable man to take part in public affairs in several centuries.

This great statesman was born in Ireland and educated at Trinity College, Dublin. There he was an average student, for he did not reveal in his youth the extraordinary powers which were later to vault him to world reknown. For a time he studied law, a discipline which was to help him in later life, but he chose not to complete his studies in that field. Burke next turned to literature, where he quickly met with success. He produced a model of philosophical criticism entitled, *The Sublime and Beautiful*, which received such high praise that it became a university textbook. But he turned from this field also, despite his obvious talent, for he felt a great compulsion to enter the political field. There, he believed, he could contribute some much-needed improvements.

Burke entered the House of commons when he was thirty-five years old. This was no small feat, but he was aided by Lord Rockingham, who was then prime-minister, and whose attention had been drawn to this young man of political promise. The Parliament at that time was a body of the elite; its members have been described as chiefly fox-hunting squires and sons of nobles. On the whole they were an aristocratic group who were fairly ignorant of public affairs, seeking further gain for themselves rather than for the nation.

At the time Burke entered Parliament, it was absorbed in the relations to the American Colonies which it was trying, under the misguided leadership of King George III, to coerce into complete subjugation. Burke began his career by opposing government policies of high taxation, no representation, and complete domination of its lands in the New World. His oratory rang out in the House of Commons as the most stirring and thrilling ever to resound in that famous hall. He stood for reconciliation, the repeal of some taxes, and the withdrawal of obnoxious restrictions and monopolies. In his speeches, Burke rightly predicted the consequences of the high-handed treatment shown to the Colonies by saying, "If you cannot reconcile your sovereignty with their freedom, the colonists will cast your sovereignty in your face." Though he did not prevail, time was on his side and his predictions came true when the American Colonies overthrew the yoke of British authority.

Later, when this issue was no longer dominant, Burke turned his attention to the dealings of Britain in India, where he opposed the tyranny his government was inflicting on that nation. He was deeply distressed by the misery suffered by the vast multitudes of Indians. He saw their land being abused by his own country, and recoiled at a private company unscrupulously bleeding Indian wealth. It was patently obvious that English courts established in the Colony of India were not meting out justice; Indian laws and customs had been rejected in an arbitrary and rough-shod manner. For his sterling efforts in seeking redress for a wronged people, and for his attempts to eliminate obvious corruption and greed, he was opposed by many powerful forces who sought to destroy him. While he was speaking in Parliament with great eloquence, his foes were using every means to destroy him. It is a tribute to his character that he was not dissuaded from his course of seeking political morality in the face of the slander and contempt directed at him.

From India, Burke next turned to Ireland and sought to overcome the ill-treatment accorded the Roman Catholics in that land. This was, in turn, followed by his overwhelming interest in the

French Revolution. While he believed wholeheartedly in reform, he was unnerved by the rejection of religious belief and the acceptance of the work and writings of such an infidel as Voltaire. He was revolted by the blasphemies and bloodshed becoming so widespread in France. What may have been Burke's greatest literary masterpiece came from his revulsion against the crimes and excesses of that revolution when he wrote, *Reflections on the French Revolution*. The work has been praised as the most eloquent and masterly political treatise ever written. His total aim in writing this volume was to encourage the establishment of justice, to condemn the wrongs being perpetrated, and to strengthen the hand of those who were trying to do right. This was characteristic of the man. Because of his moral character, he towered majestically above the other statesmen of his time. His strength lay in the proclamation of the truth, fearlessly stated and courageously defended.

Sir Edmund Burke goes down in history as one who led his generation in every worthy reform. His support brought great hope to those who fought against slavery, to the abused Roman Catholics in Ireland, to debtors subjected to inhumane treatment, to those trying to reform the courts, and to those who opposed the financial mismanagement in government. And always his presentations, whether oral or written, were based on the highest political and moral wisdom, making him an ideal to be studied and emulated to this day.

Walter Lippmann once said that the term, "statesman," is one term which, when not "used as mere pomposity, connotes a man whose mind is elevated sufficiently above the conflict of contending parties to enable him to adopt a course of action which takes into account a greater number of interests in the perspective of a longer period of time." Burke embodied this loftier view of the true statesman. It is evident in his declaration that "the state ought not to be considered as nothing better than a partnership in a trade of pepper and coffee, calico and tobacco, or some other such low concern, to be taken up for a little temporary interest and to be dissolved by the fancy of the parties . . . It is a partnership in a higher and more permanent sense — a partnership in all art, a partnership in all science, a partnership in every virtue and in all perfection. As the end of such a partnership cannot be obtained in many generations, it becomes a partnership not only between those who are alive, but between those who are dead and those who are to be born." A man who considers statesmanship in such terms of high trust is beyond question a man who applies his morals to his work in parliamentary halls.

With Sir Edmund Burke, religion and morals were not only sparks that inspired him, they lit the flames of his passion, leading him to shine as an example of great statesmanship for all the world to see and to emulate.

# Michael Faraday

(1791-1867)

Michael Faraday was born in London, England where his father was a blacksmith. His early life was one of extremely limited circumstances. The family lived in a small residence and the father, due to poor health and infrequent jobs, was barely able to support the family. Michael had little formal education. He described what education he had as being "of the most ordinary description, consisting of little more than the rudiments of reading, writing and arithmetic." Yet he became an example of how self-education can propel one into the company of the most learned people on earth.

As a youth Faraday became an errand boy and later an apprentice to a bookbinder, a Mr. G. Riebau. Taking advantage of the opportunity thus offered in his place of work, he became an avid reader of the pages he bound, picking up considerable knowledge of the subjects he thus could study and learn. In all his reading it was electricity which drew his greatest interest and ultimately absorbed him. One of the bookbinder's clients was pleased to see the boy giving rapt attention to an article on electricity in an encyclopedia he was binding and gave him tickets to the lectures of Sir Humphrey Davy, one of England's greatest and most renowned scientists. Typical of his resourcefulness, young Faraday took careful notes at the lectures, then illustrated his notes and sent them to Davy with a request for a job. The ploy worked and he was made an assistant to the great scientist.

This, in turn, brought to the young man a further boon, namely the opportunity to travel rather extensively with the great scientist. On these trips Faraday met many of the great scientists and other outstanding personalities of his day. Faraday spent fifty-four years at the Royal Institute of Great Britain where, at the age of 43 he was made research professor of chemistry. His life was thus a fairy story of one who rose from poverty and meager education to become one of the great educators and scientists of his era, with a lasting place in fame and history.

As he matured and applied himself diligently to scientific research, young Faraday made discoveries of electromagnetic induction, revealing the principle of the dynamo and electric motor, the transformer, and the telephone. He is credited with having conceived the physical idea from which radio and the theory of relativity have been deduced, and with being a pioneer in the field of electrical engineering. His place in the history of electrical science is apparent from the application of the term "Faraday's Law" to the relationship between electricity and the combining power of a chemical element. Far ahead of his time, he was the first to liquify many gases, thus providing the fuel for modern-day rockets, and for his outstanding achievements, he was honored with membership in the Royal Society. Clear proof of his extensive knowledge and authority as a scientist came one evening when, at the last minute, a man scheduled to lecture before scientists at the Royal Institution became intimidated by the reputation of the scientists gathered to hear him. He backed out of the assignment, whereupon Faraday, without preparation, stepped in and gave a scholarly lecture which was applauded by the learned gathering.

In a wide field of creativity, Faraday made lasting contributions to science. He is responsible for the terms "anode," "cathode," "ion;" he created the forerunner of the cinematograph; he discovered benzene which is the basis of the synthetic dyestuffs industry; he invented new kinds of optical glass. In working with magnets he made possible the generator, the dynamo and the magneto. And his discoveries in the field of electricity are considered the basis for all progress in that area of human achievement.

Faraday was also a deeply religious man. He was a devoted member of a sect, which has since disappeared, known as the Sandemanians. This was a very conservative religious group, proclaiming the literal interpretation of the Bible as one of its basic tenents. Faraday never missed Sunday worship and was an elder of the London congregation, at times even filling the pulpit as a lay preacher. He had been led to this sect by his grandfather, Robert Faraday, who lived in England during the times of the great evangelical religious revival generated by John Wesley. Caught up in the movement, he had veered toward this small sect, the

Sandemanians. It was this grandfather who brought to bear upon Michael the influence of this group whose teachings played such a large part in Michael's development. This religious group believed strongly in the separation of church and state. In its literal interpretation of the Scriptures, it reinstituted the Agape or love feast, as its chief ritual. It emphasized the Word of God as the norm for all of life, and demanded that its followers seek to imitate Christ in daily life. The sect grew rapidly for a time, aided by circuit-riding preachers. However, it never became widespread geographically, remaining largely a religious phenomenon in Scotland.

Sandeman, its founder, taught universalism, or the salvation of all humankind through Christ's atoning work on the cross. Footwashing was practiced. Other-worldliness was stressed to the point where members were urged not to collect wealth, but rather to be generous to the poor. The sect taught that it, alone, was the one true church; it insisted that its youth marry only within the church's membership. Excommunication was considered tantamount to being driven out of God's favor. While Sandeman's religion was one of personal relationship to Christ, he referred to God, everywhere present in nature, as The Great Cause, who not only created the world, but who also governs it. Faraday stated his belief that faith leads to as many spiritual discoveries as science does in the laboratory.

True to his religious convictions, Michael married inside the church, to Sarah Barnard. She appears to have been a perfect match for him and their home life seemed to be ideal. Their home was a place where Faraday could relax from the stern discipline of his studies and enter into either a peaceful enjoyment or participation in a happy, social function. Never having children of their own, their home was a place which their young nieces delighted in visiting. There they were entertained by the great scientist giving demonstrations of various, universal, chemical reactions, or by his collections of frogs and other specimens. It was his annual custom, at Christmas, to give scientific lectures to children.

Faraday published many of his lectures, becoming widely known as a scientific author. His publication, *The Chemical History of a Candle* written for children, has been called the first book on science written in basic English. It was translated into many languages. Although he became widely praised as as great scholar and scientist, there is no indication that such renown turned his head. He did not hesitate to reject some honors that came his way, declining, for instance, the offer to be knighted, as well as the offer to become president of the Royal Society.

In addition to his achievements in the realm of science, Faraday was an able philosopher. He was intrigued by the relationship of man to external reality. His interest in this subject, as well as his interest in the study of time, another of his obsessions, was due to the influence of Bishop Beckeley. Some of Faraday's essays are still in existence, dealing with imagination, particularly its moral implications.

As he entered the last decade of his life, Faraday began suffering periods of loss of memory, a fact which he not only recognized, but which led him to resign his appointment as lecturer in the Royal Institution. His last years were made comfortable by Queen Victoria, who provided him with a home in which he was to pass the remaining nineteen years of his life. As he lay on his death bed he was asked "What are your speculations?" He replied that he was resting on certainties, not speculation. And then he quoted Saint Paul from the Scriptures, "I *know* whom I have believed, and am persuaded that he is able to keep that which I have committed unto him until that Day." It is reported that his daily life had always been governed absolutely by the Bible.

Having declined the privilege of burial in Westminster Abbey when it was offered, he was laid to rest in a private ceremony, in a grave marked simply by his name, date of birth, and date of death. He who had been a close friend of John Tyndale, widely acclaimed British physicist, of Prince Albert, consort to the Queen, and a host of world famous scientists and men of letters, carried through to the end the spirit of his religion, seeking the blessing of God rather than the praise of men.

# Samuel F. B. Morse

(1791-1872)

Samuel F. B. Morse has been described by the single word "versatile." The term is aptly applied, owing to the achievements of this man in four different fields. First, Morse won international recognition as a painter. To this he added the career that made him most famous, that of innovator in the field of electromagnetic telegraphy and creator of the Morse code, widely used throughout the world in his day. As his financial fortunes rose, Morse showed acumen as a businessman. And finally, he engaged himself actively in the political activities of his day.

At one time, it was stated that two-thirds of all successful men and women recognized for their greatness by their inclusion in *Who's Who in America* were minister's children. Samuel Morse was one of these, born in a parsonage in Charleston, Massachusetts on April 27, 1791. His father, a staunch Calvinist, was an outstanding geographer as well as a cleric, and was distinguished as the author of the first geography ever printed in America. In addition, he had published numerous other works, such as a history of New England and a biography of George Washington. He was a trustee of both Phillips Academy and Harvard, sending his young son to Phillips when Samuel was only seven. Known by his second name, Finley, rather than Samuel, the young Morse did not give a good account of himself at Phillips. He early gave evidence of a characteristic which stayed with him throughout his life, that of being less interested in books than in art, less in strictures than in creativity.

But his pious parents did manage to develop in him some strong religious feelings. His father was a leader in the struggle to maintain Harvard's adherence to a strict Calvinist theology, and both parents exerted sufficient religious influence to induce two of their sons to enter the ministry. An insight into the religious feelings of young Samuel appears in a letter which he sent to his two brothers, students at Andover Academy at the time

Samuel was home on vacation during his senior year at Phillips:

*I now write you again to inform you that Mama had a baby, but it was born dead and has just been buried, now you have three brothers and three sisters in heaven and I hope you and I will meet them there at our death. It is uncertain when we shall die, but we ought to be prepared for it, and I hope you and I shall.*

From Phillips Academy young Morse went to Yale, though only fourteen years of age. But though he had studied hard in order to be admitted, he did not make the most of his opportunity in New Haven. Hunting was a strong distraction from his studies. However, one subject fascinated him. That was the course on electricity. He even assisted in experiments on electricity in the laboratory and independently in his room. But his room took on another atmosphere also as he made various designs for murals, which he put on his walls, along with a number of paintings. When his art work impressed his fellow students, they asked him to paint their portraits. Soon he had a steady income from these efforts, and his talent as a portrait painter came to light. Thus, the two areas in which he was later to become famous, electricity and painting, were clearly outlined in his early personality and labors. Temporarily, he did considerable carving in ivory as well.

As the time came to leave New Haven, Morse was convinced that his future lay in painting. He drew considerable inspiration from Washington Allston, proclaimed the greatest American painter of that day. Though his parents objected strenuously and, with much insistance, prevailed upon him to work for some months in a book shop, they finally allowed Samuel to carry out his dream to go to England and study under Allston, who was spending considerable time there. In England Morse met a number of the greatest painters of the era, as well as William Wilberforce, some illustrious editors, and Samuel Taylor Coleridge with whom he formed a close friendship. In the company of talented artists, Morse quickly brought his ability to full development. He won the gold medal offered by the Adelphi Society when he submitted a carving a painting accepted for display in an exhibition sponsored by the Royal Academy was judged to be among the best of the six hundred on review. Morse had now become so completely devoted to painting that he wrote, "My ambition is to be among those who shall rival the splendor of the fifteenth century; to rival the genius of a Raphael, a Michaelangelo, or a Titian." This was heady talk for a young man, but not without some justification. By the time he returned shortly thereafter to America, his works were drawing considerable praise from the greatest artists of Europe. His father welcomed him with a complete change of heart, and instead of opposing his son's ambition as an artist, he encouraged it and even rented a studio for him.

But as he worked at his art, another interest developed, much to his parents' delight. Sunday church schools were just being introduced among the New England churches and one was opened in his home town of Charleston, Massachusetts — the result of the interest and effort of a Yale roomate at Morse's brother. Drawn into a discussion of its need and benefits, Samuel was prevailed upon to become superintendent of the newly opened Sunday church school and became active in the life of the congregation. So strongly did the interest in religion grow in Morse that he gave serious consideration to becoming a minister. While he was struggling with this decision for several months he produced, with his brother Richard, a device called the Morse pump, to be used chiefly on fire engines. Versatility was now making itself obvious in his character and thinking, and causing a problem. It made him waver between a choice of several professions: painting, the ministry, architecture, and scientific inventions.

The final decision, not surprisingly, was for art, but the other interests continued to interest him greatly throughout his life. Within the field of art, portrait painting was to receive his chief emphasis and to bring him his greatest fame. An example of this reputation as a portrait artist was his commission to paint a portrait of President Monroe. For this task he spent a month in the White House in close association with the President and Mrs. Monroe, and the president was highly pleased with his portrait. Portraits of other famous people included Eli Whitney, Noah Webster, Supreme Court justices, and even Lafayette. Morse's fame was enhanced when he founded the National Academy of Art, serving as its president for a number of years.

We have said that versatility well describes Samuel F. B. Morse; this trait now came to the fore. In spite of the fact that he was immersed in his work as a painter, alongside his passion for art another interest was growing in his mind. It sprang from his earlier studies in the laboratory at Yale when his interest in electricity had been strong. Morse was now toying with the idea that an electric spark could be used to send telegraphic messages. It was an idea that a few other scientists had already suggested but Morse was unaware of this fact. He followed through in the development of the idea, and out of this effort there developed the famous Morse Code, which would soon become the standard means of communication around most of the world.

Now New York University appointed Morse to a professorship in "the literature of the arts of design." On that campus, among other things, Morse experimented for several years with the perfection of a telegraph. He brought together a team of men interested in its development, and they were of considerable help to him. They made numerous changes as one attempt after another failed to produce the perfection sought. Finally, Morse presented an outline of the machine to the patent office, and a few months later asked the government to accept the invention and establish a system of telegraphy for the United States. There was considerable delay while the matter was discussed in congressional committee. During this time Morse, true to the diversity of his spirit, followed still another interest — this time in the picture-taking process originated by Daguerre, known as the daguerreotype. Morse and the inventor became close friends, working together on the process, earning Morse the reputation as a famous Daguerreotypist. This early process in the history of photography was the subject of widespread interest.

Finally Congress passed the bill authorizing the establishment of a telegraphy system. Morse was jubilant as he became officially the superintendent of United States telegraphs. When the first line was stretched from Washington, D. C. to Baltimore, Morse, with his religious background, sent over the wires from one city to another the famous first message, "What hath God wrought?" Morse was later to see his work produce transoceanic communication, as lines were laid across the waters from New York City to London. Through association with the developing telegraphic business, he was to rise from a long life of near poverty and frequent begging to the status of a man of means. Nine nations of Europe, using his telegraphic instrument, met and agreed to unite in paying him a handsome sum of money. Several scientific societies honored him with membership, and Yale University awarded him an honarary doctorate. Morse was now as well known internationally in the world of science as he was in the realm of art.

Young Morse had also held strong political convictions. His father was an ardent Federalist, but young Morse with his staunch adherence to Jeffersonian principles, disappointed his father by taking opposing views. He was encouraged in his views during his stays in England and later in France, as well as through his friendship with Lafayette. The father was outspoken, as well, in his religious views as a leader in opposing the liberalism rising among theologians in the East, and especially at Harvard. Now young Morse got involved in a dispute that involved both politics and religion. For a time, this was to engage all his energy. The controversy sprang from a growing resentment among Easterners toward the surge of foreigners arriving on American shores. Called Nativists, these native Americans were appalled at the vast numbers of people arriving from abroad. Among this huge influx of immigrants were large numbers of Roman Catholics, and a strong anti-Roman feeling rose in America. Morse was for a time caught up in its emotions. The newly enfranchised people from abroad were reportedly selling their votes to city political bosses. Morse entered the fray with his pen, publishing, among other works, one entitled *Foreign Conspiracy Against the Liberties of the United States.* His opposition to Roman Catholics was political and not religious, and he refused to enter into theological disputes. Morse's interest and efforts in the cause culminated in his nomination for mayor of New York City on the Native American ticket, but of four candidates for the office Morse finished last. Four years later, he was again nominated for mayor, but at the last minute withdrew his name. Later he ran for congress on the Democratic ticket, but for the third and last time lost in his quest for political office. Morse did, however, remain exceedingly active in politics, writing about his views and raising funds to support the nomination of those with whom he agreed.

The spiritual side of Morse's life was clearly evident. Always religious by nature, many of his spontaneous exclamations were quotations from Scripture. When his parents were informed by his letter that he would be marrying the girl of his choice he wrote,

"Praise be the giver of every good gift." As the day for their wedding approached, Morse wrote to the intended bride, Lucretia,"Our blessed Savior honored a marriage supper with his presence, thereby giving countenance to all the joys of the occasion." Throughout his lifetime Morse engaged in daily devotions, frequently seeking to persuade others to his religious faith. At a great gathering, on the evening of the day when a large statue of Morse had been dedicated in New York City, the aged inventor was asked to sit at a telegraph on the stage and send his "last message." Typical of Morse, the message clicking out from the key for all to hear concluded with, "Glory to God in the highest, on earth peace, good will to men."

# Florence Nightingale

(1820-1910)

Often a family will produce a child who shows singular characteristics not shared by parents or siblings. Florence Nightingale
was one of these children. Hers was a selfless spirit, rejecting what
could have been a life of ease and luxury. This is the more remarkable when one understands her mother and the kind of family
atmosphere in which Florence was raised, for it was said of her
mother that to her, material things came first in life. Born of
wealthy parents, she loved society with its parties and various
social events; she delighted in owning large houses in which she
enjoyed the attention of maids, valets, coachmen, and footmen.
She enjoyed travel but doted on her two mansions where she gave
elegant parties for large numbers of guests. One of her homes held
fifteen bedrooms, but she considered it too small for entertain-
ing. Such activities were conducted at Lea Hurst, already large
when she moved in, but to which she added six more bedrooms
at the time her two daughters were introduced to society. All this
lavish luxury was said to have spoiled her sister, Parthenope, but
it did not spoil Florence. Indeed, such surroundings had the op-
posite effect, leading Florence to consider how shallow social life
and indulgence in material means can become.

Young Flo was pretty, intelligent, quick to learn, and gifted
with leadership qualities. She readily grasped mathematics, and
considered taking advanced courses in that field. She gave evidence
of possessing the mind of a scientist by seeking precision in everything and in her thoughtful consideration to every detail of
whatever she was studying. But she revealed, as well, a depth of
character which led her to reject what she called "useless trifles"
in order to seek "something worth doing." As a young girl she
enjoyed the company of a kindly vicar, who liked children, and
who encouraged her interest in the healing of farm animals, dogs
and other pets. Her father, who had a sensitive nature, encouraged
the development in her of a love of people and a caring interest

for the injured — even a concern for trampled plants or flowers. Since the vicar enjoyed company when making his visits on parishioners, he took Florence with him. She heard him offer words of cheer to the sick and bereaved, listened while he gave advice on the use of medicines and dietary foods and made suggestions about nursing care and hygiene. It is believed that this time spent with the caring vicar had a strong influence on the young girl.

At seventeen Florence conducted a Bible class at Lea Hurst for the girls who were employed in the hosiery mills. With no interest in the empty, social life offered her, and with a burning desire to render selfless service to humanity, she was utterly frustrated by the prejudices of the day which prevented a woman from freely pursuing her basic interests. Once she was known to have exclaimed, "Oh, God! What is to become of me?" It seemed to echo the sentiment of the sainted Apostle Paul who had declared, "Woe is me if I preach not the Gospel."

Florence's upbringing and education included not only music and art, like many young ladies of her day, but also literature, science, and training in Italian, French, and German sufficient to make her fluent in all three languages. In addition, she travelled widely through Europe and in Egypt, and had been invited to royal court on several occasions.

Much of what is known about the inner thoughts of Florence has been gleaned from her notes, written from time to time throughout her life. Though somewhat like a diary, these notes were less a record of events than a transference to paper of her deepest, philosophical thoughts. Thus on February 7, 1837, she wrote, "God spoke to me and called me to His service." It would be several years later that she would feel sure of the type of service into which he was calling her, but that date was the start of a continuing sense that she was destined for some special work in the service of humankind.

While her mother was a social butterfly, Florence's deeper, altruistic spirit would seem to be a throw-back to preceding generations of her family, in which such dedication was apparent. Her great-grandfather, for instance, had been known as a humanitarian for his interest in helping the unfortunate. Her grandfather, in turn was a member of the House of Commons, where he established a reputation as a champion of the poor and neglected. And her own father showed considerable understanding of the ideals that were moving and inspiring his daughter.

Out of this background, Florence developed a clearly defined attitude toward material wealth. Instead of taking pride in the impressive home in which she lived with her parents, she thought of its possible uses outside the family. Once, when walking on the lawn with a friend, she looked up at the huge mansion and said, "Do you know what I always think when I look at that row of windows? I think how I should turn it into a hospital, and just how I should place the beds."

One can imagine the effect on the socially involved parents, especially her mother, when Florence informed them that she wished to become a nurse. To them, such activity was on the level of the lowest of household servants, and far beneath her social and educational status. Thus, it was no easy task for Florence to make the decision, inform her parents, and then stick to her resolve. On the one hand her mother was greatly influenced by social standing and public appearance and acceptance; on the other hand, most hospitals were a mere shadow of such institutions as we know them today. Only the sick who could not afford home care were herded into such institutions, or those whose need for surgery demanded the use of such facilities. Hospitals were considered spreaders of germs, and they were badly overcrowded, often dirty, and plagued by offensive odors. They even carried the stigma of immorality, as people questioned the presence of a woman at physical examinations or when surgery was in process. A doctor of that day reported, "most of the nursing is done by drunken prostitutes who, when brought into the police court, are given the option of going to prison or to hospital service . . . They are often found in sleep under the beds of their dead patients whose liquor they have stolen." One can easily understand why there was strong belief that a "lady" should not nurse one of low social standing. So Florence was breaking new ground and it was a formidable task.

But, while her mother lacked understanding of the high ideals that were motivating her daughter, Florence found encouragement from her aunt Mai, sister of her father. As Florence turned away from frivolous pursuits, she turned toward this understanding aunt, who not only sympathized with Florence's idealism, but who became, as well, a spiritual mother to her niece. An insight into the high idealism and spiritual nature of Florence is revealed by a statement she wrote when still a young girl, "I craved for some regular occupation, for something worth doing, instead of frittering away time on useless trifles." Like some others of wealth, before and after her, who turned from their material abundance because of a desire to help the poor, Florence, at the age of twenty-two wrote, "My mind is absorbed with the idea of the sufferings of man, it besets me behind and before . . . all that the poets sing of the glories of the world seem to me untrue. All the people I see are eaten up with care of poverty and disease." Still later she wrote, "O God, Thou puttest into my heart this great desire to devote myself to the sick and sorrowful. I offer it to Thee." With such emotions and desires stirring within her, it is not surprising that finally, at the age of twenty-four, Florence was persuaded that the call from on high was to enter into hospital routine in order to care for the sick. Knowing the overwhelming opposition of her parents, she delayed an entire year before informing them. Their reaction, especially that of her mother, was as expected. Their utter rejection of the idea was accompanied with so much anger and disgust that another eight years passed before she entered the profession. Her family's attempt to remove her absorption in services of mercy led them to provide opportunities for extensive travel to other lands.

But this tactic merely played into Florence's hands, for on such journeys she managed to locate institutions dealing with humanitarian needs, and to study their programs. In Egypt she enjoyed viewing the sphynx and pyramids, but sought out the Sisters of Saint Vincent de Paul. In Greece she viewed the ancient ruins, but investigated, also, an orphanage under the sponsorship of American missionaries. Later she studied the French Sisters of Mercy in Paris, closely observing their program of nursing and care of the sick. Thus, she was engaged in a practical course of study in the field of her professional choice.

It was her fascination with the care of the sick and elderly that induced Nightingale to visit Pastor Theodore Fliedner at Kaiserworth, Germany. There this Lutheran Pastor was pioneering his Institute for Deaconesses, which was to become famous for its training of women in nursing and other avenues of religious service. Florence was so impressed that she published a booklet about the Institute, which was later to establish the Deaconess program among Lutherans of North America. She later returned for three months of rigorous training at Kaiserworth.

On a tour of Italy, Nightingale spent ten days in the Convent of the Sacred Heart at the *Trinita dei Monti*, a Roman Catholic sisterhood devoted to education and the care of orphans. Thus it was a series of contacts with religious institutions which fed her interest in human welfare and led her to follow that Christian interest with singular devotion.

Finally, after years of frustration, the door was opened for Florence to launch the career which would make her world-famous. An institution in London bore the impossible name, The Institution for the Care of Sick Gentlewomen in Distressful Circumstances. In short, the facility was a nursing home for women of limited means. It had come to Florence's attention that this institution was to be completely reorganized and was seeking a new superintendent. So in 1853, by which time Florence had gained stubborn independence, she secured the backing of an influential friend and applied for the position. It was offered to her, but only after considerable discussion, remuneration to consist of living quarters but no pay. Thus Florence, though lacking in experience, launched upon an administrative career as a pioneer in nursing.

In this position, her brilliance quickly became evident. So, too, did her commitment. She plunged into the reorganization with zeal, bringing forth new and original ideas. She saw that the institution should be moved, and worked out the details of relocating it on a much more favorable site. Because her work was branded a success, she could have considered her accomplishments here to fulfil her long-sought goal. But larger goals were haunting her, and she moved on to other positions of authority in institutions caring for the sick. All of England seemed to her to be desperately in need of an efficient and well-organized program of nursing. And, indeed, it was. Nightingale was inspired to lift nursing to the level of a profession, caring for the sick with great competency and much dignity, encouraging people with talent to join the profession.

Her opportunity to bring much respect to the profession arose suddenly as the result of a national catastrophe. England was at war in the Crimea, fighting against the Russians; in the process of gaining a decisive victory, there were many thousands of

English casualties. It was a great shock to the English people when they learned through newspaper accounts of the piteous treatment of their wounded soldiers, and of their neglect due to the lack of proper nursing personnel. Army nursing corps had not yet been invented; that day was still a far cry from today's uniformed medical branch of the services. Newspapers in England were severely critical not only of the fact that the wounded lay unattended for as long as a week, but also of the fact that there was "not even linen to make bandages." As a result of strong public opinion, and strong sympathy for the troops, the army decided to open up avenues of nursing services for women. To organize and superintend the first corps of women nurses, the government turned to Florence Nightingale. On October 21, 1854, she led the first contingent of thirty-eight nurses to the Crimea. There she once again proved to be a genius in her organizational and creative responsibilities. Her work was publicized in the newspapers which spread her fame throughout the land. However, this, in turn, aroused some jealousies and led to attempts to detract from her achievements. But at this stage in her life, Nightingale's reputation was strongly established, and even Queen Victoria came to her defense, sending her a letter of commendation.

Just how desperate the situation was in the hospital in Scutari can be learned from Florence's own words,

> There are no clean shirts . . . the men have only rags saturated with blood . . . The hospital has been transformed from a barrack and underneath its imposing mass are sewers loaded with filth, through which the wind blows fetid air up the pipes into the wards where the sick men are lying. Wounds and sickness, overcrowding and want of proper ventilation contribute to the foulness of the atmosphere . . . The wards are infested with rats, mice and vermin. Flooring is defective; furniture and even the commonest utensils for cleanliness, decency and comfort are lacking . . . The vermin might, if they had but unity of purpose, carry off the four miles of bedding on their backs and march with them into the War Office in London.

Taking into account Florence Nightingale's severe shortage of critical materials, and the overwhelming numbers of sick and wounded to be cared for by her small band of nurses, her results in treating the wounded soldiers were truly miraculous. Her achievements could only be attained through an unusual devotion to her task. The manner in which she even used her influence to gain the cooperation of authorities, and the lengths to which she went to gain proper provisions and facilities for handling her charges, comprise a story in themselves. Let the size of her achievements be illustrated by the report in the London Times, detailing how within only a few days, she put in order two hospitals, containing three or four thousand patients. She was not only an efficient nurse, she was an extraordinarily proficient hospital administrator. Her personal involvement with the patients knew no bounds, and perhaps even more significant than her physical ministrations to the sick was her contribution to their mental and emotional welfare, as she revived their hopes and their determination to recover in spite of their present sordid circumstances. Late at night or early in the morning, when she was not tied down with clerical and administrative duties, she would make long tours of the wards, giving special attention here and there to those who were extremely wounded. The men so appreciated the unusual dedication of this woman, whose heroic efforts were almost the only hope for their survival, that they would kiss her shadow as it fell across their pillows and then relax.

Lord Ellesmere, in an address to the House of Lords, stated that "dying men sat up to catch the sound of her footsteps or the flutter of her dress, and fell back content to have seen her shadow as she passed." Later, when she became deathly ill with a fever which she contracted in caring for the troops, the news of her serious illness struck England as though it were news of a defeat in battle. Her subsequent rallying and then recovery were greeted with relief, not only by the common people of her homeland, but by even the Queen. In a letter to the Secretary of War, Queen Victoria expressed her thankfulness "to learn that that excellent and valuable person, Miss Nightingale, is safe." There was no doubt that she had now become a national hero. But, significantly for this study of religious motivation, even the Queen was moved to refer to this hero's "Christian devotion." And in a speech to raise funds for a fitting national recognition of Nightingale's labors, Lord Stanley said, "The best test of a nation's moral stand is the kind of claim which it selects for honor. And with the exception of Howard, the prison reformer, I know of no person besides Miss Nightingale who, within the last one hundred years within this Island, or perhaps in Europe, has voluntarily encountered dangers so imminent, and undertaken offices so repulsive, working for a large and worthy object, in a pure spirit of duty towards God and compassion for man."

Also among this remarkable woman's many and diverse talents was her ability as a writer. Despite her other activities, she found time to produce and publish material on the field of nursing. One book on the subject became so popular that thousands of copies were sold and the volume was translated into three foreign languages. In her last years, when Nightingale was less active in other areas, she undertook a prodigious writing assignment. Among her works there appeared the three-volume title *Femina Sum (I am woman)*, in which she combined her religious faith and modern ideas to inspire women to realize the fulness of their responsibilities as human beings.

Not to be overlooked among her contributions to hospitals and the recovery of the ill was her success in introducing proper food and diet to the menu. In spite of objections of "higher ups" who considered the items "preposterous luxuries," she insisted on seeing that the patients were given such health-giving items as soups, with wine added to increase strength and appetite, and jellies to make their trays more appealing.

At the close of the war it seemed that Florence Nightingale's work would be at an end, but such was not the case. By now her position as an authouity on nursing was so well established, that various men in high government positions kept up a constant correspondence, soliciting her suggestions on a wide variety of questions regarding health and sanitation problems — particularly in the armed forces. She was even the originator of a cost-accounting system for medical services in the army, so efficient that it became the official procedure to be followed for nearly a century.

One can readily see that modern nursing is the product of Florence Nightingale's career. Before her time, those who tended the sick were recruited from charwomen or those of lowly status, and society actually looked down upon the work of those hired to perform hospital chores. Florence raised nursing to the level of a profession, highly respected, requiring considerable, specialized training, talent, and a motivating desire to serve. She brought to it the element of dedication. Her work was, to her, God's work. "Nursing," she said, "is an art; and if it is to be made an art requires as exclusive a devotion as any painter's or sculptor's work; for what is the having to do with dead canvas or cold marble compared with having to do with the living body, the temple of God's spirit?"

In the closing years of her life, the honors conferred upon her included the Order of Merit, received from King Edward VIII, an outstanding honor since she was the first woman ever to receive it. She was given, as well, the honor known as the Freedom of the City of London. These were but two of many forms of recognition given to her for her lasting contributions to humanity. Still, not all honors are those bestowed by governments, or conferred in the limelight of great publicity. Perhaps Florence Nightingale's recognition lies in the remarkable increase in the choice by parents of the name of Florence for their daughters, for as a result of Florence Nightingale's reputation and fame, her first name moved from being one seldom chosen to that selected by thousands of parents who wished to honor the "lady with the lamp."

For all her high honors, including public recognition by Parliament and personal decorations by the King and Queen, Florence remained a humble person. Her thoughts were of service to others, not recognition for herself. She lived to be ninety, and by then had become so famous that there was considerable public opinion that she should be given the distinctive honor of burial in Westminster Abbey. But Nightingale had expressed the wish that she be given no special honors at death, and she was buried in the family plot at East Willow, where her tombstone bears the simple inscription, "F. N. Born 1820. Died 1910."

# Louis Pasteur

(1822-1895)

Louis Pasteur, widely proclaimed as the most important single figure in the history of medicine, was born December 27, 1822 at Dole, France and he rose to greatness from a humble heritage. His parents were intelligent people of good reputation, his father a tanner, his mother the descendent of a family of gardeners. Pasteur's father left the tanning business for awhile in order to serve his nation in the Napoleanic Wars. There he distinguished himself by receiving the Legion of Honor medal in recognition of special bravery.

As a boy, Louis showed considerable talent for painting, especially portraiture. One of his first paintings was of his mother, whom he pictured as she went out one morning to market, wearing a white cap and blue and green Scotch plaid shawl. Because of his ability in this field, it was generally concluded that Pasteur would spend his life as a portrait artist. But at the age of sixteen he decided against a career in art.

He attended the Royal College of Besancon where, while earning his Bachelor of Science degree, he excelled in mathematics but, surprisingly, not in chemistry. Yet, he was destined to be known as the greatest chemist, and later, biologist, in France; and he pursued his study of chemistry at the famous Sorbonne. Shortly thereafter Pasteur became a teacher of chemistry at Strasbourg, and so began his great career in that field. At Strasbourg the Rector, a Mr. M. Laurent, had a daughter, Marie, with whom Pasteur immediately fell in love. They were married in 1849 and it proved to be a very happpy marriage. His wife adapted well to Pasteur's great obsession with science and the scientific laboratory, encouraging and supporting him in his endeavors. They were well known as an ideal couple and well matched.

In 1854, at the age of 32, Pasteur gained recognition in the academic world by his appointment as a professor at the University of Lille. This was really the start of his intensive research, conducting experiments that would bring him first much con-troversy, then wide acclaim. He became the founder of microbio-logical sciences and brought to humankind some of the greatest benefits of modern science. It is not possible to count the number of lives saved as a result of his discoveries, and still millions more have been relieved of suffering because of him. Among his greatest contributions are the theory of polarization of light, knowledge of the action of fermentation, the discovery of airborne germs, the treatment of rabies and hydrophobia, and the introduction of innoculations producing immunity in people (and cattle) to vari-ous diseases. And he is credited with saving the chicken industry in France. More will be said of this later.

Every housewife is familiar with the term "pasteurization," and is aware of its benefits. By the introduction of the pasteuri-zation method of killing germs, he aided the beet sugar industry, as well as wine producers, and above all, the dairy industry which was able to make cow's milk safe for babies, thus saving count-less infant lives.

Pasteur's first success as a scientist was in the field of chemi-cal minerology. He became widely recognized as an expert in the field of crystallography, and his election to the Academy of Science in Paris was in the section on minerology. But Pasteur branched out into many areas, achieving remarkable results. He is credited with founding the science of bacteriology. After proving the exis-tence of microbes, he then went further to discover that some were harmful while others were beneficial to humanity, and he learned how to deal with each. Although he did not develop the germ theory of disease, he championed it so vigorously, backed by so much irrefutable scientific proof, that he was able to con-vince scientists of its correctness. He discovered the existence of organisms in the air which cause liquids to ferment and which can cause infection in wounds; this led to his advocacy of antiseptic surgery, which the famous Dr. Lister was to successfully spread throughout the world of surgery.

In 1865 Pasteur was asked to study diseases of the silk worm, which had become so rampant that the entire silk industry was threatened with extinction. He responded by establishing a labora-tory in the center of the area where the trouble was greatest. There he not only developed techniques that led to the rapid recov-ery of the silk industry, but discovered also the cause of the epidemic, so that the future of the industry was assured.

In 1879 Pasteur turned his attention to an epidemic disease which was then raging among chickens. This led him to discover the means, through vaccination, of overcoming chicken cholera and anthrax. Thus Pasteur was able, on several occasions, to be the man of the hour — uncovering the cause for diseases which were threatening humanity's stewardship of fowls, silk-worms, and cattle.

Pasteur also experimented with mad dogs, and so discovered a serum which was effective in their cure. He had developed a system of innoculation that could save farmer's herds of cattle; now he was sure that the same method would be effective in humans, but, naturally, hesitated to take risks with human life because of the possibility of blundering. The risk was truly enormous, as it was not known how strong the injected serum should be. Finally, when a child, Joseph Meister, bitten by a mad dog, was brought to him, Pasteur knew the dying boy had no hope at all unless the serum could save his life. Pasteur administered the serum, carefully following his best judgment; then followed three weeks of terribly anxious waiting, but the treatment proved effective and Pasteur was credited with this great discovery that would save human life, and bring him much fame throughout the world.

History has witnessed a recent increase in the longevity of human life, and the contributions of Pasteur deserve much credit for bringing out the substantial decline in the death rate which followed his discoveries. Though they may not know it, many people now living owe a substantial debt to this brilliant man. Sir William Osler spoke for the realm of scientists when he said of Pasteur, "To no man has it ever been given to accomplish work of such importance to the well-being of humanity." Evidence of his continuing recognition as one of the greatest contributors to the advancement of science is found in a poll of school children in France. When asked to name the greatest man on the list of Who's Who in French History, the children did not vote for an emperor, like the colorful Napoleon, nor a soldier of fame, like Foch, nor for any other statesman or scientist or religious leader. Their outstanding choice was Louis Pasteur.

Nevertheless, though he was one of history's greatest scientists, Pasteur never accepted the scientific theory of evolution arguing that life springs from already existing life, pointing unmistakably to a Creator. But Pasteur was also a man of positive, religious faith and was unashamed to state this fact anywhere, at anytime. This was most clearly demonstrated when he was inducted into that famous assembly of outstanding scholars, the French Academy. Its head was Ernest Renan, well known as a free-thinker. The young Pasteur was not cowed by him. Standing in the presence of Renan, as well as before the other learned members, Pasteur boldly proclaimed not only his faith in the Ultimate Being, but his belief that such faith is natural to the human heart. He is quoted as saying, "Everywhere in the world I see the expression of the idea of the Infinite. Owing to it, belief in the supernatural is found at the bottom of every heart . . . Science and the passion for knowledge . . . what are they but the spurs which the mystery of the Universe applied to our souls?" He once admitted that he prayed constantly at his work in the laboratory. He continued his remarks before the Academy by declaring, "No one can escape admitting the existence of the Infinite. I see everywhere in the world the inescapable expression of the Infinite. As long as the mysteries of infinity weigh upon the mind of man, so long will temples be built for the worship of the Infinite . . . And upon the mosaic pavement of whose temples you will find men kneeling, prostrate, overwhelmed with the thoughts of the Infinite."

Pasteur had a solid reputation as a man of great moral fiber and strength of character. He was a man with a strong spiritual life imbued with lofty ideals: honesty, love of truth, unselfishness, willingness to sacrifice self, nobility of character. He believed that spiritual values transcend science. Indeed, he was driven to his discoveries not by a desire for fame and recognition, but by a deep love for humanity, a desire to bring cures to the afflicted, but also a feeling of deep love for these people as individual humans. It is said that he suffered with his patients. Pasteur was praised highly as one who practiced "the Gospel virtues," and who "reverenced the faith of his fathers." He once described how it was his study of the mysteries of Nature that contributed to his faith; as he died he is said to have reached out for the comfort of that faith, and in it died with peace and calm. He had spoken of himself as a believer in immortality, and once told some college students that among the factors responsible for his success was "an instinctive leaning towards all that is fine and noble." Those who have written his biographies have been unanimous in praising his moral virtues, painting him as a man of singularly beautiful ideals and high aspiration. In a famous cemetery in France is a plain stone monument with a brief inscription: "Here rests Pasteur." Nothing more is needed. Any attempt to condense into a few words the enormity of his contribution to life would be futile.

# Count Leo Tolstoy

(1828-1910)

Leo Tolstoy, destined to become one of the unique figures in history, was the fourth of five children born to his parents in Czarist Russia. He was only two years of age when his mother died, and as he grew, he often questioned those who had known her about his mother. From their complimentary statements he came to think of her as a saint, and he developed an unusual attachment to her memory. Throughout his life, he would frequently fantasize that he could talk to her and that she would console him.

Tolstoy was born to nobility, amid much wealth, and was raised on a large estate. There was much pomp and outward show to the life within his home. Dinner, for instance, was a dramatic event; the doors to the dining room, closed until dinner was ready, would be ceremoniously opened by a servant who stood at attention as the family entered the room. At the table was a servant assigned to each chair, serving a single individual throughout the meal. The diners engaged in lively discussion of various topics, and the mealtime was a period of considerable gayety and joy.

Amid all this luxury and attention, Leo grew up somewhat spoiled, engaging in such excesses of youth as drinking and gambling. But as he left his teens Tolstoy was converted into a young man who desired to transform the world into the image of Christ, stressing Christian brotherhood and love. He developed a particular concern for the peasants who worked the landed Tolstoy estate, seeking to better their economic conditon, and improve their life through education. He had a natural bent for writing, and already in his early twenties was widely known for his essays on his personal experiences. Titles of his books during this period include *Childhood, The Invaders, Boyhood, Recollections of a Marker, The Woodcutting Expedition, Sevastopol in December, Sevastopol in May,* and *The Cossacks.* All these works enjoyed wide circulation, and their appearance in rapid succession established his reputation as a prodigious writer. In fact, he was something of a phenomenon in literary circles.

Reminiscent of St. Augustine, Tolstoy passed through the excesses of youth to become remorseful, determined to change his ways and begin a search for truth in morals and religion. He became an enemy of hypocracy and insincerity, strongly opposing all sham and artificiality. He has been described as a youth who was full of humor, lively, sensitive and kind-hearded, and who sometimes carried these qualities to the extreme. Thus, when he developed a deep aversion to the traditional, wanting to choose his own path and free his talents for creativity, he discarded formal religion, though he was then only sixteen. Soon, however, and throughout the rest of his life, religious and moral zeal burned within him.

Tolstoy was only nineteen when he inherited from his father's estate the village of Yana Polyona. It is said that he plunged into the opportunity to help the peasants here, and that he considered it a sacred duty to care for the best interests of the 700 villagers. Thus Tolstoy tried to improve their lot by applying various theories of farming and agriculture, and by establishing a school in which he taught. His own education was furthered when he studied oriental languages and the law at the University of Kazan.

Leaving school, Tolstoy spent several years engaged in various military assignments, but did not advance in rank beyond lieutenant. He was judged to be a good leader, with military inventiveness, but his love of personal freedom did not endear him to his superiors. Leaving the military, Tolstoy traveled for a year, broadening his outlook and expanding his knowledge of people and society. At the same time he developed a gross disgust for the artificiality and materialism of life, as he witnessed it in his day. Tolstoy became an idealist who believed that humanity's real life begins when the spiritual forces in us triumph over our animal nature and materialistic goals. After a year of travel, Tolstoy returned home to begin a life of service to the peasants on his large estate.

Tolstoy's philosophy of life was apparent in his famous works, *War and Peace,* and *Anna Karenina,* in which he attacked life's problems and sought solutions. In producing these works he became a national hero and won world-wide acclaim. *Anna Karenina* has been given the highest possible praise, sometimes called the greatest novel ever written, and classified with such timeless works as *The Aeneid*. His complete works, published after his death, run to ninety volumes. Even his famous rivals had to acknowledge his superiority; Dostoyevski declared that Tolstoy was superior to any living novelist, while Turgenev called him the "great author of the Russian land." His novels and short stories have been translated into many languages for distribution throughout the world. Several have even received a wide distribution through film a century after they were written.

Music also had a great appeal for Tolstoy, so much so that he gave serious thought to making it his full-time occupation. He excelled at the piano and possessed considerable ability as a composer. This strong interest in music remained with him throughout his entire life. Turning from the fancy of a career in music, Tolstoy directed his attention instead to forestry and farming, largely as a result of his desire to help the residents of the village which he had inherited.

But the main thrust of Tolstoy's writing was concerned with his religion. Here he was a paradox, at the same time a devout Christian and a religious skeptic, believing in Christ but doubting the promise of life after death. This attitude made the death of his especially beloved, older brother a shattering experience for him. Several times Tolstoy thought he was in love and one of the most serious of his romances ended over their disagreement on religious convictions. He had an unusually complex reaction to spiritual matters, making it difficult for some people to understand him.

While his creative talents first led to the introduction of some progressive theories of education, these same talents led him also to question the meaning and purpose of life. This in turn led him to religion, where he came into contact with a thought that was to play a large part in his thinking for the remainder of his life — Christ's command to "resist no evil." This discovery has been called the pivotal point of Tolstoy's conversion; thereafter, much of his energy and work were devoted to books and articles on moral, ethical, religious, and social themes. He propounded the thesis that the best literature is that which "infects" the greatest number of people with the loftiest feelings of love, brotherhood, and compassion. His books of this period, dominated by a religious and humanitarian spirit, include *What I Believe, The Kingdom of God is Within You, Kreutzer Sonata, Resurrection,* and his dramas *The Power of Darkness, and The Living Corpse.* Tolstoy was constantly influenced by these two dominant beliefs: that Christianity is a faith to be translated into action, to be actually lived; and the doctrine of non-resistance.

As a Bible critic, Tolstoy refused to accept a literal interpretation of Scripture, but was convinced that in the teachings of Christ one might find an explanation of the purpose of life. A pragmatist, he underscored five rules for life which he credited to the teachings of Christ: (1) control your temper; (2) do not lust; (3) refuse to be bound by oaths; (4) do not resist the evil one; (5) follow the spirit of doing good to all people, both the just and the unjust. From these basic principles, Tolstoy derived the inspiration for almost all of his interests and writings during the last half of his life; and because of them, became a critic of certain practices in both church and state. Tolstoy attacked the concept and practice of private property, of war, of smoking, of drinking alcoholic beverages, and even the eating of meat. He became an outspoken pacifist, preached charity, and declared that the ills of society would disappear only when all people learned to love one another.

Opposed vigorously by the church, Tolstoy was excommunicated in 1901. Thereafter, his work in the field of religion was largely published abroad, then smuggled back into Russia. He thus gained a reputation as a moral philosopher, and became known not only as the greatest of novelists, but also as "the conscience of the world." His followers came close to founding a religious sect under the name of Tolstoyism, but he opposed such formality, believing that the Kingdom of God within each person would manifest itself in various ways, as each individual strives for perfection. It was the striving, rather than attainment, that Tolstoy urged, for he believed perfection to be an unattainable goal to guide our striving.

Tolstoy's abhorence of materialism in later life nearly caused him to reject the world and all its goods. Following the Apostle Paul's concept of tent-making ministry, he wished to be entirely self-supporting. He worked in the fields with the peasants, and with his own hands made many items of personal clothing including his boots. Royalties from his works became suspect to Tolstoy, and he desired to turn this income over to charity, but his wife persuaded him to deed much of this income over to her, to be held in trust for their children. Her success came only after much bickering which led to an estrangement between husband and wife.

It had been at the age of thirty-four that Tolstoy married Sofia Andreyevna Bers, and judged that the first fifteen years of their marriage were the happiest of his entire life. Thirteen children were born to this marriage. But in later years there was trouble between husband and wife due largely to some of Tolstoy's rather strange decisions. Then, as old age approached, and Mrs. Tolstoy became concerned about their financial future, their occasional difficulties led to a complete estrangment. Tolstoy withdrew from her and finally left the home secretly at night. He was to die shortly thereafter, away from his wife, but with some of the children at his side.

Tolstoy's religious beliefs were subject to constant change for, such was his nature, and he would frequently surprise his wife with some startling change in his social habits. After his death Tolstoy's wife remarked, "I lived with Lev (Leo) for forty-eight years but I never recall learning what kind of man he was."

Tolstoy was an inconoclast, railing against many practices of the church of his day, refusing to accept all facets of orthodoxy; yet, at the same time, he was a zealous missionary, preaching a doctrine of love, forgiveness, and dependence on a boundless God. Thus, some would view him as a saint, others as a menace to religion. He became an object of scorn by the religious hierarchy when he attacked them in his book, *The Resurrection,* which was widely read and acclaimed — and which led to his excommunication from the Russian Orthodox Chruch. The book was primarily a satire of the courts and the deficiencies of the criminal justice system. But the ills of society, including the many sweatshops, and the hypocricy he found in the church, also faced his attacks. Tolstoy's description of the Mass conducted in prisons, and the priest who presided, is reminiscent of Luther's exasperation with some Roman priests whom he witnessed racing through the Mass.

Practicing what he preached, Tolstoy gave all his possessions to worthy causes and was ultimately to die a pauper, having renounced his titles and the land to which those titles gave him possession. The 80,000 rubles received from publishing *The Resurrection,* which immediately became a best seller, he donated to help the Dukhobers emigrate to Canada. But the book was discussed widely both in Russia and in other countries. The Church was stung by the portrayal of weaknesses within its ranks, and since Tolstoy was known to deviate from the apostolic faith, they publicly denounced him, then excommunicated him.

Tolstoy was Unitarian, believing in God as "the Spirit, Love and Principle of all things." He strongly urged a life of prayer for all who could come to know God. He believed that Christ was the greatest example of God's will, "but to regard Christ as God, and to pray to him, is to my mind the greatest possible sacrilege." He underscored the doctrine of non-resistance of which he believed Christ to be the supreme example.

Although some of Tolstoy's views contradicted basic tenets of apostolic Christianity, he was inspired by his religion, and there is no doubt that Tolstoy believed God to be an ever present reality asking man to seek to conform his life to the way of godly love. Tolstoy taught that Christianity was a practical religion, a faith to be lived, and felt himself to be a part of the God who had created him.

Tolstoy has been called a Christian anarchist . . . because he opposed organized religion. This stance resulted from his opposition to the rigidity of the dogmatism, to the heavy-handed tactics of the church of his day, and to what he saw as deception in the church. Tolstoy did, however, as has been noted, believe strongly in God, in a moral universe, and accepted the then neo-Christian teachings which opposed the materialistic life. Throughout his lifetime Tolstoy often spoke of one's sacred duty to God, and engaged in a lifetime search for truth. Though he turned from the church for a time, he came back to it with a zeal, worshiping in his native town while under a church ban. The purpose of his work was to stress the absolute necessity of religion, and it is beyond denial that this man, one of the greatest writers of all time, drew inspiration and wisdom from his religious faith. It was this faith which provided the spark for his search for truth — and which lit the path along the way.

# Andrew Carnegie

---

(1837-1919)

This great philanthropist was born into modest circumstances in Scotland. His father was a weaver, operating a hand-loom in his own home. He had three other looms beside the one he operated, and these were run by either hired help or other members of the family. Following the economic trends of the day, the family alternated between periods of prosperity and of want. Looms had been in operation for a number of years, but their time now was short, for the use of steam power was beginning to spread. This quickly resulted in the replacement of cottage industry with larger mills. Andrew's father was among those thus affected.

Andrew was another of those famous men who owed a great deal to the influence and philosophy of his mother. From her he learned to remain optimistic in the face of adversity. She sang hymns of hope, engaged the family in prayer, and led the family in Bible reading, encouraging each family member to memorize favorite passages. She also bred in Andrew a love for honest toil and a hatred for slothfulness.

When Andrew was eleven, the family trade had completely failed, so his father decided on a bold move. They would move to the New World, where he believed he could manage to support his family. They chose to settle in Pittsburgh, where two of Andrew's aunts on his mother's side lived, and from whom the family had heard that there was opportunity for work. The ocean voyage to New York consumed seven weeks, followed by spurts of travel on railroad and canal to Pittsburgh. Immediately upon arrival, Andrew's father secured a job in a cotton mill, and even Andrew, though only 12, went to work in the same factory, spending twelve hours a day at his job. A year or so later, Carnegie was helped by a friend to become a telegraph operator for the Pennsylvania Railroad. There his talents caught the eye of Thomas A. Scott, Superintendent of the Railroad's Pittsburgh Division When Scott became president of the Railroad, Andrew Carnegie succeeded him in the Superintendency.

But this is getting ahead of the story. An incident in young Andrew's life, during his employment at the cotton mill, reveals one reason for the boy's rapid advancement in life. It begins with James Anderson of Allegheny who owned a library of four or five hundred books, and who decided to open his library to the public. Taking advantage of this opportunity, Andrew Carnegie started reading and did not stop until he had read every book in the collection. This love of books and learning was a foretoken of the later Andrew Carnegie who would donate two thousand libraries to cities and colleges. Just as he was an avid reader, so Carnegie was a diligent student of whatever was at hand, and he was creative as well. He caught Mr. Scott's attention when he demonstrated that an economy of words could speed the process of telegraphy. Forwarding a message for Thomas Scott, Carnegie signed it Tomscot. Mr. Scott was delighted with this ingenuity and took young Andrew under his wing; as Mr. Scott ascended the ladder of success he constantly brought Carnegie up behind him. It was Scott, while serving as Assistant Secretary of War under Abraham Lincoln who appointed Andrew Carnegie Superintendent of United States Railways and Telegraphs.

But Carnegie branched out on his own, as well. He helped to organize the Woodruff Sleeping Car Company, which was later bought by the Pullman Company. He was shrewd enough to invest in profitable oil lands which he later sold for several hundred thousands of dollars. He foresaw the need ultimately to replace America's wooden bridges with spans made of iron, and organized the Keystone Bridge Works. When he saw the need to make iron rather than import it from Birmingham, England, Carnegie went abroad to study the Bessemer process of making steel, and upon his return started manufacturing the Bessemer steel railroad track. Already well-to-do, Carnegie rose to his position among the outstandingly wealthy men of the world on steel rails. He was an astute businessman and had learned how to realize a large return on borrowed money. As a result, he could continually enter new ventures and make the gamble yield big dividends.

But as his personal wealth skyrocketed to huge proportions, Carnegie constantly increased his generosity by supporting worthwhile activities. He believed it a sin for a person to amass great wealth and die without having given substantial support to positive causes. So, as Carnegie grew rich, many cities and colleges received libraries, science halls, and music centers. The famous Carnegie Music Hall in New York became a reality, and because of his love for Bach's music Carnegie donated pipe organs to churches, schools and halls. He supported generously the New York Oratorio and the Philharmonic Society. As his great spirit of philanthropy became widely known, Carnegie began to receive requests for financial support from all over the world, as up to five hundred requests for money a day arrived at his desk. Almost always his gifts proved the seed money for larger enterprises. That is, he would give only when the parties pleading for funds would themselves provide a portion of the means for reaching their goal. Money never turned his head, and so he remained humble, explaining his attitude toward money as follows:

> The day is not far distant, when the man who dies, leaving behind him millions of available wealth which was free for him to administer during life, will pass away unwept, unhonored and unsung, no matter to what use he leaves the dross which he can not take with him. Of such as these the public verdict will be, "The man who dies thus rich dies disgraced." Such, in my opinion, is the true gospel concerning wealth, obedience to which is destined some day to solve the problem of rich and poor, and to bring peace on earth and good will to men.

On another occasion Carnegie restated this position:

> The aim of the millionaire should be, first, to set an example of modest, unostentatious living, shunning display and extravagances; to provide moderately for the legitimate wants of those dependent upon him; after doing so to consider all surplus revenues which come to him simply as trust funds which he is called upon to administer, and strictly bound as a matter of duty to administer in the manner which in his judgment is best calculated to benefit the community. The man of wealth thus becomes the mere agent and trustee for his poorer brethren, bringing to their service his superior wisdom, experience and ability to administer, and doing for them better than they could or would do for themselves.

In spite of his generosity, Mr. Carnegie's personal wealth continued to rise. As his personal value reached two-hundred-fifty million dollars, new causes received his attention. For instance, believing that those in the teaching profession were not sufficiently paid, he established the Carnegie pension fund for retired teachers, with an initial gift of fifteen million dollars. But while he helped large groups of people in society, he always retained a personal touch. He knew by name the many people who headed the various divisions of his enterprises, and kept in touch with them. A shrewd judge of character, Carnegie was interested in helping young men make good. This was the purpose of his philanthropy which enriched technical schools, for he believed these schools would develop character by helping those of the lower classes to learn to make a living with their own, developed skills.

Toward the end of his active life Mr. Carnegie was involved in an unbelievable number of large and flourishing enterprises. In addition to those already mentioned, his empire included oil, ships, coal, and coke. He was interested in many different business endeavors and he reached out in all directions, though all his enterprises were inter-related, each proving useful to the others. All in all, Carnegie displayed unusual, and seldom rivaled, ability as an executive, creator, and investor.

Thus a life which began in a devout home, influenced by a praying mother who stressed character, produced a great man of industry, an outstanding philanthropist, and a man whose friends admired him as an avid reader and student of political and economic history, literature and philosophy, psychology and architecture, and as a lover of poetry, art and music. Here, indeed, was a man worthy of emulation.

Carnegie's religious stance has been misunderstood by some. He has even been called an atheist. But a closer look reveals a man whose spirit was in tune with the highest religious principles. Though he had little regard for theology, Carnegie was clearly an adherent of the basic Calvinistic theology in which he was raised. He searched for truth in his wide readings and associations with men of keen minds, and he promulgated that truth. He donated to churches, and in full measure exemplified the Good Samaritan of Christ's parable, striving always to be a good neighbor and to lift up his fellows.

# Sanford Ballard Dole

(1844-1926)

So many people have heard of Dole pineapple that it is natural for them to think of Mr. Dole as a great industrialist, amassing much wealth by raising, canning and shipping boatloads of delicious pineapple throughout the world. Most people do not realize that Dole was the son of dedicated missionary parents and that, as a public figure, he gave himself with great devotion to the islands of his birth. Admitted to the bar, he practiced law for many years, and during a part of that time served in the Hawaiian Legislature. This was followed by a series of extremely important positions, including that of Justice of the Supreme Court of Hawaii, president of the provisional government, president of the Republic of Hawaii, first Governor of the Territory, (after he helped gain its annexation to the United States), and finally, Judge of the Federal District Court of Hawaii. Far from being limited to the role of wealthy industrialist, Dole was an outstanding figure in the political history of Hawaii. His leadership came at the time of Hawaii's miraculous transition from an isolated tribal culture to a modern industrialized society. All this transpired within a century and reached fulfillment when Hawaii became our fiftieth state.

As a part of the Sandwich Islands, Hawaii began to attract missionaries to work among the Polynesians around 1830. Showing the usual zeal of missionaries, and with great dedication to their work, they were able to replace idol worship with Christianity. At the same time, the missionaries' efforts resulted in the replacement of grass huts with buildings of stone and wood. Soon schools were established, winding trails gave way to paved roads, industries arose, and sea-going vessels began arriving in Honolulu Harbor from all over the world.

Among these early missionaries playing an important role in Hawaiian history was the family of Sanford B. Dole. They left their beloved New England behind them in the spring of 1841 to help plant the Christian faith in this faraway island. Their first son was born in Hawaii, and two years later their second child, Sanford was born on April 23, 1844. Four days later the family suffered the loss of the mother who was unable to recover from childbirth.

Growing up in missionary circles, Sanford Dole came under strong religious influences which were to exert their effect upon him for the rest of his life. His father and step-mother had hoped that he would become a minister, and for a number of years he mulled this possibility. But in his Senior year at Williams College he made a final decision to study law. Even so, Dole chose the legal profession with a strong impulse to be of service to humanity. His parents tried to dissuade him from entering law school, thinking the ministry offered greater opportunity to serve mankind. But the young Dole wrote them "Law is, I trust, only to be the channel of my life's work, God and humanity the ends toward which I work, and self last. The office of a true lawyer as a peacemaker is second only to the office of a minister." The spirit in which he chose his life work undoubtedly explains the self-sacrifice with which he later dedicated himself to a series of public offices, and which led to his historic contributions to the development of Hawaii.

When Sanford's father, Daniel Dole, arrived in Hawaii as a young missionary in 1841, there was a crying need among the missionaries for a school. Since none were available the parents had only two choices. One was to let their children grow up without formal education. The other was to suffer the emotions of seeing their little ones, as soon-to-be first graders, board ship and travel far from home in order to attend a school in the United States. Though the missionaries had enough to do in establishing churches and carrying on their church work, they decided to found a school as well. The decision was made just as Daniel Dole was arriving in Hawaii. Since a superintendent had to be chosen for the new school, and Daniel Dole was a well-educated man, he was the immediate choice for the position. Thus, he was thrust at once into the double duty of preaching and academic administration. However, the result was an emphasis within his home of both religion and education. Perhaps this explains the life-long interest of Sanford and his brother George in various subjects of educational importance. George's interest lay in collecting rock specimens and an interesting assortment of shells. Sanford took such an interest in birds that he was able to make valuable contributions to the famous Harvard museum, publishing a number of articles on the subject. Dole's talent as a writer became evident when he edited a newspaper for several years, during his early law practice. His paper was constantly furnished with well-written articles from his own pen on a wide variety of political and educational subjects.

Sanford's boyhood was pleasant; he and his brother, George, were constant companions at school and work and play. The work, tending an extensive garden plot, filled many of their hours and fed the family; later they worked on nearby plantations. The play included horseback riding and trips to various parts of the island with their father. They enjoyed the sea, as well, and spent many hours in the surf or swimming in the blue water. Their ability as swimmers was tested one day when their small boat was upset several miles off shore, forcing them to swim against strong currents as they made their way to land. When one of Sanford's friends heard of the incident he paid tribute to Sanford's ability as a swimmer, commenting that he would as soon expect to hear that a fish had drowned as Sanford Dole. In addition to all these activities, the two brothers hunted a great deal. It was through these hunting expeditions that Sanford became interested in wildlife. He followed this interest through with much reading on the subject until he became a recognized authority on Hawaiian birds.

When Sanford had finished the course offered in the school of which his father was superintendent, he attended the college which had been founded by missionaries at Puhahou. This was several hundred miles from his home, and could be reached only by ship. This was the prelude to a separation, by a much greater distance, when he traveled to Williams College in Massachusettes for the final year of his college education. The ocean voyage was unique in several respects.

The long journey from Honolulu to New England in those days was in stark contrast to today's relatively easy trip. It was an ordeal that consisted first of the sea voyage to San Francisco, then by ship again to Panama, through the Panama Canal, and up the Atlantic coast to New York. Until the time of Sanford's departure for Williams College, only sailing ships had stopped at Hawaii. However, during the year 1866, when he made his

journey the radical change from sail to steamship was realized between California and the Islands. The pioneer ship of the California Steam Navigation Company, on which he rode, was the *Ajax*.
Among its passengers on its first stop in Hawaii was the young
Mark Twain.

The year at Williams College provided a great variety of experiences for Sanford Dole. His studies were concentrated in the
sciences, including zoology and anatomy. During that year the annual elections for class-day honors became embroiled in controversy. Among the results was the resignation of the president
of the senior class. Proof of Sanford's leadership ability is shown
by the fact that, in only his third month on campus, he was elected
president of his senior class. But there was also a fierce struggle
within Sanford himself, as he wrestled with the choice of a life
career. In the end he came to the decision that he should study
law, though he knew it was the strong wish of his parents that
he become a minister.

The decision to become a lawyer meant that Sanford would
have to spend another year in the States, a much shorter period
of study than now required of law students. There was a friend
of the family, Senator Brigham, who had a law office in Boston,
and who invited Sanford to study law with him. It was a fine
opportunity, and Sanford accepted the offer.

Boston was known for its culture, and the young law student made full use of the opportunity to visit museums and
libraries. One of his good friends, whose acquaintance he made
there, was Edward Everett Hale who rose to national fame as
the author of the book, *The Man Without a Country*. He was
fortunate in meeting one of the great figures in literature, Charles
Dickens, as well, and took pride in writing home about this experience.

Upon the completion of his study of law, Sanford Dole passed
the bar examinations and returned to Honolulu where he began
his practice of law in the office of Judge Hames W. Austin. The
young lawyer set up bachelor quarters in which he lived for four
years until his marriage, in 1873, to Anna Cate. The marriage
proved to be a congenial one, though Anna was forced by poor
health to leave Hawaii twice for recuperation, and the couple was
never able to have children.

Hawaii's first king was selected in 1871, but the one chosen,

Lunalilo, died after little more than a year on the throne. Because his successor was a man of major weaknesses, Dole decided to run for the legislature, feeling he could thus contribute to the development of good government. Dole became a leader of the minority party, gaining sufficient prominence to be later appointed a justice of the Supreme Court. In that position he showed such outstanding talents that other public honors came in rapid succession. When public disatisfaction with the high-handed tactics of royalty led to the rejection of monarchial government, Dole was chosen as president, in 1893, of the newly established provisional government. He began immediately to work for the annexation of Hawaii to the United States. Four years later, his efforts met with success when Hawaii was annexed to the United States, and Dole was elected the first territorial governor. He held this position for five years until his retirement in 1903. Thereafter Dole was looked upon with honor as an elder statesman, respected not only in Hawaii but by nations and governments of the world. He left a lasting moral and political imprint on his beloved land, working for the recognition of Hawaii as one of the United States. After his death, Dole's dream came true.

# Theodore Roosevelt

(1858-1919)

The twenty-sixth president of the United States was born in New York City on October 27, 1858, and died at Oyster Bay, New York on January 6, 1919. A man of varied talents and interests, he was scholar, explorer, soldier, writer, and president. As President of the United States he expanded the powers of that office and of the federal government on behalf of public interests, whether in fighting crime or in the conflict between big business and big labor. He was a dynamic leader, and consequently became a controversial figure. But he was also one of the most popular and important occupants of the White House.

The second of four children, Roosevelt suffered poor health as a pale and sickly child, afflicted with an asthmatic condition, and defective vision. Because of his health he did not attend school, but received private tutoring of such high quality that he was able to enter Harvard where he won scholastic honors. He was able to emerge from his frail condition to enjoy a robust manhood by means of vigorous exercise. Horseback riding, boxing, target shooting — all became part of his active life, climaxing in mountain climbing and safaris. But such activities were paralleled with much reading and mental stimulation, and at Harvard his scholarship won him membership in the high scholastic fraternity, Phi Beta Kappa. During his college years, Roosevelt became interested in military affairs, conducting the research for a book published a year after his graduation, entitled *The Naval War of 1812*.

Teddy Roosevelt's entrance into politics came when he was elected to the New York State Assembly at only 23 years of age. During his three terms in the assembly, Roosevelt was influential for one so young, and even led the minority group of Republicans in the passing of some reform bills. He then spent three years in the operation of a cattle ranch in the west before returning to New York City to run for mayor; but the campaign was not successful. His disappointment over his defeat was assuaged, however by his marriage to his childhood sweetheart, Edith Kermit Carow. This was his second marriage, his first wife having died suddenly just two years after their marriage. He and Edith became the parents of four children, one of whom, Kermit, became prominent in military affairs.

For a few years, Teddy stayed out of politics, playing the roles of scholar, writer, and sportsman, and traveling considerably. He came to love the West, writing and speaking about it often, but he was restless for an opportunity to re-enter politics. That opportunity came in 1889 with his appointment to the United States Civil Service Commission by President Benjamin Harrison. He was later reappointed by President Cleveland. For six years he served as chairman, gaining publicity by campaigning vigorously to eradicate the corruption which had infiltrated the system, and succeeding in uncovering a considerable amount of fraud. He fought dishonesty, not only because of immediate, degrading effects, but because he believed that the spoils system and corruption in government were making politics distasteful to many good people who might otherwise run for public office. His identification with clean government led to another assignment where he was to receive attention as a colorful person, seeking to wield the sword of righteousness in the public good. This was his appointment to the Board of Police commissioners for the City of New York.

Though there were four commissioners, the strength of Roosevelt's personality and his dedication to the work soon resulted in Roosevelt's emergence as the head of the commission and its undisputed leader. Many stories have been told of the ardor with which he plunged into the work of cleaning out corruption from the City's "finest." His zeal for this task had been developing ever since his days in the state legislature, where he had been involved in a legislative investigation into a number of questionable practices by the guardians of the law in the nation's largest city. Roosevelt had urged the introduction of civil service, and a change from four commissioners to one. But now, eleven years later, his appointment brought him into the middle of a situation which was as bad as when the need for reform was first publicized. Roosevelt would ride around at night with a member of the police force, or walk his beat with him, in order to see first hand what needed to be done, or to catch an officer in wrongdoing. Roosevelt would frequently take a newspaper reporter with him, as well, in order to make certain there were disclosures of the incidents he was fighting to eliminate. As a result he received generous publicity in big city newspapers all over the country. His zeal for enforcing the law made him many enemies, not only among the criminals and corrupt officials, but also among a much larger populace when he rigidly enforced the prohibition laws of the City, and its rule for closing businesses on Sunday.

Roosevelt's growing reputation in politics was enhanced in 1897 when President William McKinley named him Assistant Secretary of the Navy, and it is said that he soon began to over-shadow the Secretary of the Navy. As an outstanding orator Roosevelt was frequently required to make speeches in which he called for a more powerful navy, and suggested that the United States should intervene in Cuba's revolution against Spain. When Congress declared war against Spain in 1898, Roosevelt resigned from the Navy Department and accepted a commission in the Army. Within a short time, he had advanced in rank to Colonel and his outfit became known as the Roosevelt Rough Riders. The high point of this rather short war was Roosevelt's leadership of his command in the famous charge up San Juan Hill in the face of intense enemy fire.

It was largely Roosevelt's colorful leadership in the war that led to his nomination for the governorship of New York on the Republican ticket. During his tenure as Governor, he coined the popular phrase; "speak softly but carry a big stick." His record in that office has been referred to as the best in the history of the State. He stressed a sense of public trust among his fellow offi-cials. He sympathized with the underpaid teachers and secured salary increases for them. His love of God's out-of-doors led him to work for measures aimed at saving the wildlife and preserving the forests and natural beauty of the state.

From the governorship, Roosevelt moved into the vice-presidency, because his party was not pleased with his lack of cooperation with their state machine. He and McKinley won the election, but the president was assassinated just a few months later, leaving Roosevelt the presidency.

His record as president stands clearly revealed in many works by various authors, but space here will not permit a lengthy enumeration of his many achievements. It is sufficient to say that as president he fought the power of the big trusts, continued his strong interest in wildlife preservation, and ended the threat of a strike by 140,000 members of the United Mine Workers union. But in his own mind, it was the building of the Panama Canal which was his most important contribution as president; it was at his strong urging that Congress passed the necessary legislation to negotiate for the construction of the canal. One last achievement must be mentioned. Roosevelt determined to act as mediator in the Russo-Japanese War which had been in process for more than a year, and because he was able to bring together representatives of the two nations, inducing them to reach an agreement, he was awarded the Nobel Peace Prize.

Roosevelt's first term in office, lasting three and one-half years, was followed by his election to a full term. He decided not to run again, and President Taft succeeded him in office. But four years later Roosevelt vented his displeasure with the manner in which Taft was dealing with big business, and so decided to run again as a third party candidate. It was an unsuccessful effort, and Teddy retired from public affairs.

His religious beliefs had a strong influence upon Roosevelt's presidency. He believed, for instance, that racial discrimination was morally wrong, and that it threatened the life-strength of any nation. He was a close friend of the famous black educator, Booker T. Washington and relied upon him to recommend well-qualified blacks whom he appointed to various positions in government. He disdained the criticism hurled at him when he entertained Mr. Washington at dinner in the White House. Roosevelt made known his views on many moral questions of his day, more so, perhaps, than any other man to hold that office. Such topics as women's rights, marriage, divorce, and birth control were all subjects of his pen and tongue. Speaking of the nation's prosperity, or lack of it, he observed that "against the wrath of the Lord the wisdom of man connot avail." He boosted the mission activity of the churches, stating his belief that "Christian missions have for their objective not only the saving of souls but the impacting of a life that makes possible the kingdom of God on earth." The breadth of his faith was revealed in his concern for the church attendance of laborers, in his recommendation of religious books for general reading, in his interest in the office of chaplain of the armed forces, and in his concern over the declining numbers of young men entering the ministry. His intolerance of discrimination, religiously as well as racially, led Roosevelt to place both Jews and Roman Catholics in his Cabinet.

Roosevelt was quick to praise the contributions of religion to American life, and once declared:

> The whole country is under a debt of gratitude to the Methodist circuit riders, the Methodist pioneer preachers, whose movement westward kept pace with the movement of the frontier, who shared all the hardships in the life of the frontiersman, while at the same time administering to the frontiersman's spiritual needs and seeing that his pressing material cares and the hard and grinding poverty of his life did not wholly extinguish the divine fire within his soul.

Roosevelt made it plain that although a distinguished soldier, he nevertheless could say that in any question between peace and righteousness he would not for a moment hesitate to choose righteousness. He made such statements as "We must insist on righteousness first and foremost" and "I abhor war . . . But if I must choose between righteousness and peace, I choose righteousness." As a former Sunday church school teacher and faithful attendant at worship services, he knew his Bible well and often quoted it. The following is an example:

> I know not how philosophers may ultimately define religion; but from Micah to James it has been defined as service to one's fellow-man, rendered by following the great rule of justice and mercy, of wisdom and righteousness.

Roosevelt was an activist, a man of energy, whether he was involved in hunting, politics, religion or any other of his many interests. He carried this over into his religion, where he approved of the practical activism of the Social Gospel. This led him to say that

> If, with the best of intentions, we can only manage to deserve the epithet of "harmless", it is hardly worthwhile to have lived in the world at all . . . Alike for the nation and the

*individual, the one indispensable requisite is character — charac-*
*ter that does and does as well as endures, character that is ac-*
*tive in the performance of virtue no less than firm in the refusal*
*to do aught that is vicious and degraded.*

It is easy to see why a man who thought and spoke in this manner would be chosen to root out the corruption that had come
to hold New York City in its grip, and would be chosen to head
the police force with special portfolio to clean out the vice. One
would also rather expect this man of action and pragmatic religious outlook to choose as his favorite Bible text Micah 6:8,
"What does the Lord require of thee but to do justly, and to love
mercy, and to walk humbly with your God?" One is not surprised
either that he wanted the church, which he loved, to march for-
ward without what he perceived to be the deterrent of certain
rituals and creeds. He declared that the churches had plenty of
forces to attack without being at each other's throats.

Roosevelt's lifelong church membership was in the Dutch
Reformed St. Nicholas congregation in New York City. He was
a devout and faithful worshiping Christian, who made his religious loyalty known and who urged others to do the same. It is
impressive to read these words of one who attained the highest
office in our land, and who became a world figure;

*In this actual world, a churchless community, a community in*
*which men have abandoned, or scoffed at, or ignored their*
*religious needs, is a community on the rapid down-grade. I ad-*
*vocate a man's joining in church work for the sake of showing*
*his faith by his work. Church work, and church attendance,*
*mean the cultivation of the habit of feeling some responsibility*
*for others. Yes, I know all the excuses. I know that one can*
*worship the Creator in a grove of trees or in his own house.*
*But I also know as a matter of cold fact that the average man*
*does not thus worship.*

Roosevelt was quick to give a boost to any worthwhile religious program, whether it be the Methodist church with its circuit riders or the chautauqua programs which he praised for their
effectiveness in adult education in religion.

It cannot be overlooked that more than one biographer has
denigrated Roosevelt's theological views. He was not a strict

denominationalist. He stressed action, or good works, so strongly that the Christian emphasis on faith seemed at times to be almost
overshadowed. Yet his steadfast church attendance throughout
his life, his call to support the church regardless of the denomina-
tion, his references to the Bible, his various humane interests, and
his stress upon righteousness, lead one to conclude that in his way,
he was a decidedly religious man. It was under this influence that
he developed into the dynamic figure he was. In fact, Owen
Wister, one of Teddy Roosevelt's biographers declared, "If they
melted him down . . . to his ultimate, indestructable, stuff, it's
not a statesman they'd find, or a hunter, or a historian or a
naturalist . . . they'd find a preacher militant."

Roosevelt's combination of militant activism, and challenge
to idealism, is best exemplified in a paragraph he once wrote. It
has been duplicated in bronze and displayed in a number of college gymnasiums and field houses as a challenge to athletes. It
reads:

> It is not the critic who counts, not the man who points out how
> the strong man stumbled, or where the doer of deeds could have
> done better. The credit belongs to the man who is actually in
> the arena; whose face is marred by the dust and sweat and
> blood; who strives valiantly; who errs and comes short again
> and again . . . who knows the greater enthusiasms, the great
> devotions and spends himself in a worthy cause; who, at the
> best, knows in the end the triumph of high achievement; and
> who, at the worst, if he fails, at least fails while daring greatly,
> so that his place shall never be with those cold and timid souls
> who know neither victory nor defeat.

# George Washington Carver

(1861?-1943)

Carver is a man who deserves to be honored not only for his great accomplishments, but because he was able to achieve so much in spite of his humble origin and the many obstacles he faced throughout most of his extraordinary life. Carver was born near Diamond Grove, Missouri, the son of slaves. Accurate records of slaves and their families were not usually kept by their owners, so the exact date of his birth is not known, but is thought to be around July 12, 1861. George, however, tried to eliminate this blank in his life, and by doing some calculating decided to choose July 12, 1861 as a likely and proper date on which to celebrate an annual birthday. Because of this same lack of records it is not known how many brothers and sisters Carver had. But it is well known that he had a brother, Jim, and that the two boys enjoyed a close relationship until early manhood when Jim died during a smallpox epidemic in 1883. While George was still a small child, his father was killed, and soon thereafter kidnappers stole George, his sister, and their mother from the plantation of their master, Moses Carpenter. When their whereabouts were discovered, Moses Carpenter somehow managed to secure the return of George in exchange for a horse whose value at the time was reputed to be three hundred dollars. The picture that remains of Moses Carpenter is of a kindly man, sympathetic to the fact that George was not in good health, and willing to encourage the boy in securing an education.

Almost a mile from the Carver farm was the small Locust Grove church, which welcomed the black brothers among its white worshipers. The preaching was largely by circuit preachers, and of various denominations, thus giving George's faith an interdenominational flavor. Later he would attend an Episcopal church and still later join a Presbyterian congregation. Formal education was hard for George to attain. First, there was segregation. The Locust Grove church was used during the week as a school, and for a time George and his brother attended there, but soon there arose a clamor from some whites who succeeded in having the black brothers barred from attending the classes.

George was blessed with an extremely inquisitive mind and possessed an observant eye as well. As a result, he was largely self-taught during these early, formative years. He sought to identify every bird or flower that he saw in his frequent walks through the woods, and wondered about the cause of their coloration or peculiar characteristics. Because his "parents" were uneducated, he practically taught himself to read, though very few books were at his disposal. For a short time he was tutored by a neighbor, but then his first real break came. When he was about twelve his "parents" permitted him to live in the county capitol, Neosha, where, due to a compulsory education law in Missouri there existed a school for blacks. Neosha was about eight miles from his home, to which George returned on week-ends. Though he now began to spend much less time with the Carvers, they had made an impression on him that would last throughout his lifetime. Now, in Neosha, he came under the influence of another couple with whom he lived, Mariah and Andrew Watkins. They were black and so now became his first black "parents."

Carver gained all he could from the poorly trained teachers in Neosha and, after about two years, followed a black migration by hitchhiking to Fort Scott, Kansas. But he soon left there when the lynching and burning of a black, who was accused of rape, made an impression upon him which left scars lasting the rest of his life. The next step on the odyssey of his piece-by-piece education was at the home of a family in Olathe, Kansas, with whom he moved, shortly thereafter, to Minneapolis, Kansas.

In all these communities Carver worked at a wide variety of jobs, always handling several at one time. He did housework (including cooking), worked in a store and in a laundry, and shined shoes. In all these places he kept adding to his store of knowledge, though the educational process came in bits and pieces. In Minneapolis, where he helped a doctor by doing odd chores, he was able to borrow books from the doctor's library, which texts he eagerly devoured.

By 1885, when he was about 24, Carver finished high school in Minneapolis. This was something of an accomplishment for a black man in those days, but George had no intention of stopping there. It was his aim to go on to college. He applied at Highland College where he was accepted until, upon his arrival, it was learned that he was black and was thus cruelly turned away. Through persistence, he was enrolled, in 1890, in Simpson College in Iowa. One can imagine what the rejection at Highland College had meant to this young man, and it could have crushed his dreams, but it is a tribute to Carver's character that, when one door closed before him, he kept seeking until he found one he could enter.

To the credit of Simpson College, George was not only admitted, but his fellow students were unusually kind and generous to him. He proved his merit by being a good student despite working to help support himself. He made almost straight A's in his favorite subjects of botany and horticulture and earned better than a B average in all other subjects. Carver showed considerable talent as an artist and had planned to major in that field because of his painting ability. His art teacher took a special liking to him and appreciated his talent, but at the same time, she was deeply impressed by his interest in botany and his love of painting plants and flowers. He surprised her with his zeal for cross-breeding plants, specimens of which he brought to class to show her. She, herself, was no stranger to this field of learning, for her father taught horticulture at Iowa State College of Agriculture and Mechanical Arts at Ames, Iowa, the institution now known as Iowa State University. Through her influence, George left Simpson College after one year to start what was to be his culminating educational experience as a student at the State University. He continued to work on the side, and to earn high grades, receiving his bachelor's degree in 1894. The Ames Experimental Station employed him as assistant to a noted botanist and mycologist, Louis Pammell. Carver's thirst for higher education not yet fully quenched, he enrolled in graduate school at Ames, and in another year of schooling earned a master's degree. Now came his first full-time job. Turning down other opportunities for employment, he accepted Booker T. Washington's invitation to head the new department of agriculture at Tuskegee Institute in Alabama, where he was to devote the remainder of his professional career to furthering the education of blacks and lifting their economic level. While his genius and his outstanding talents would do much for his own people, Carver was to make many discoveries which would benefit all humankind.

Tuskegee was located in the State of Alabama, and when Carver went there to teach and experiment, he found that the land was thoroughly exhausted by single-crop cotton cultivation, eroded and sun parched for lack of plant cover. He set out at once to restore the mineral content of the soil by teaching the blacks to plant nitrogen-producing legumes. His research showed that the Alabama soil could yield a good production of peanuts and sweet potatoes, so he began to teach the farmers the principle of crop diversification. When many heeded his advice but found no ready market for their new products, he began experiments that resulted in more than 300 by-products of the peanut and sweet potato. This was an enormous contribution to the economic welfare of the area, for his demonstrations of the commercial possibilities of these drastically changed the economy of the South.

When Carver was a child he had already become interested in plants, and his interest was maintained and deepened by his learning of their medicinal value. He thus saw them as more than weeds, or cultivated plants, or merely decorations on the landscape. And this led him to a study of their nutritional as well as medical value. Later, Carver was able to make use of this knowledge in dealing with the malnutrition of the southern blacks, as well as in aiding the fight against numerous afflictions. Working with others, Carver attacked such maladies as tuberculosis, malaria, hookworm, and pellagra. In the field of dietetics he researched cowpeas, sweet potatoes and peanuts, in his desire to make up for a shortage of meat in the black person's diet.

The results of Carver's work with hybrids and different types of fertilizers were spectacular. At the experimental farm at Tuskegee he evolved a cross between tall-stalk and short-stalk cotton, which was called "Carver's hybrid," as well as several other strains. In addition, Carver developed enormous vegetables. Carver and Henry Ford worked together on many projects, and together they perfected a process for extracting rubber from the milk of the goldenrod.

Carver began a "school on wheels" for small farmers who could not come to Tuskegee to learn about soil fertilization. His movable campus and school idea was adopted by the United States Department of Agriculture and in many foreign countries as well.

Carver's desire to find uses for the useless involved a wide variety of materials. As has been stated, he was able to open up to wider use the application of fertilizers for producing better crops. Because he believed that nature produced no waste, he sought ways to use everything that grew. He advocated the making of rugs and other objects from waste plant fibers. He succeeded in using the various clays found in his locality to produce coloring that could be used in painting houses. He developed, and urged the use of, calcimine. He produced stains that could beautify the interiors of homes and developed laundry bluing and a metal polish from native materials. As a result of these accomplishments, Carver must be considered one of America's great scientists.

The results of Carver's research and the products of his laboratory became known in constantly widening circles until his name was recognized throughout the world. As a result, many people, including the renowned Thomas A. Edison, offered him employment at high salaries. However, he was not interested in money, but in simply being able to render service, so he declined the various tempting offers to leave Tuskegee. Moreover, Carver would not accept a raise in salary above the meager $1,500 per year that Booker T. Washington had offered him when he first came to Tuskegee.

Carver's first publication from Tuskegee, a pamphlet called *Feeding Acorns to Livestock* (1898) was followed by 43 other publications, adding distinction in literature to his other accomplishments. He received many honors, among these being his election to fellowship in the British Royal Society of Arts in 1916, and his receipt of the Spingarn Medal in 1923, The Roosevelt Medallion in 1939, and the Thomas A. Edison Foundation Award in 1942.

In 1941 the Carver Research Foundation was established at Tuskegee Institute. Carver gave most of his savings to the Foundation, and after his death on January 5, 1942, in Tuskegee, Alabama, his entire estate was added to the Foundation's endowment. The Carver Museum at Tuskegee, which houses many exhibits of Carver's work, was dedicated in 1941. There also stands the George Washington Carver National Monument at the site of the Moses Carver farm and the Congress of the United States took note of Carver's outstanding achievements by designating January

5 as a day to honor Carver each year.

Religion was always central in Carver's life. Before college he had attended church and Sunday church school regularly, and had felt close to God as he wandered through forest and field, observing nature in all its forms. At Ames, he helped form a group which met regularly for prayer. He was active, as well, in the College Y.M.C.A. where for two years he served as a committee chairman. He also organized at Tuskegee a very popular Bible-study group which met on Sunday evenings. Later Carver would call his laboratory at Tuskegee "God's little workshop," and would always pray upon entering it. He has been described as one whose eyes sparkled and whose soul seemed to catch fire when talking about the things of God.

For this renowned scientist of world reputation, spiritual insights applied everywhere. He looked on nature as a series of miracles; all growing things were to be revered as the unfolding of God's great and fascinating design. Rather than agree that there was any conflict between science and religion, Carver believed and taught that science revealed God. It is reported that he inspired his students to great interest in botany and agriculture by speaking to them of the miracles of nature. His religion led him to love his students, who could turn to him at any time for counseling, but crucial to his counseling sessions was discussion of the Bible.

In spite of the ill-treatment sometimes accorded him because of his race, and in spite of the many hardships he endured because of his economic status, Carver drew from his religious faith a strong trust in a just universe and a beneficent Creator. It was man, he decided, who brought evil into God's good creation. He sought to indoctrinate his students with the thought of God's love, and the renunciation of hate. They were to return good for evil. In his research, he declared that he would hold in his hand a peanut or a sweet potato and ask of God, "Lord what do you want me to do with this?"

Carver had many talents in addition to his scientific ones. He could entertain well on the guitar and taught others to play the instrument. On the campus, he would frequently be called upon to give dramatic and humorous readings. He was productive in art as well, and gave a great many of his pieces to students and faculty members. His fame in this capacity grew to the point where one of his paintings was selected to represent the State of

Iowa at the World's Columbian Exposition in Chicago. Until he was in his forties, Carver even harbored the hope of establishing his reputation in art rather than in science.

Thus, through hard work and self-education, Carver rose from a child of slaves to become a distinguished scientist, painter, writer, and agronomist, one who greatly advanced the social and economic welfare of the world. Equally pronounced was Carver's virtue as a humble and deeply spiritual man, who constantly witnessed to his faith.

# Mahatma Gandhi

(1869-1948)

Here was a rather simple man who used simple means to become known throughout the world as India's most outstanding
citizen. He was a man of peace, deeply influenced by religion, who,
by means of non-violence, brought freedom in various forms to
his native land. He was born October 2, 1869, son of a prime
minister in the small princely state of Porbandar. His mother,
deeply religious, was adored by her son. In fact, Gandhi openly
credited his character to his mother's influence. He was a mis-
chievous lad, however, who excelled in some studies and did
poorly in others. Although he believed he had no gift for learning, he was nonetheless able to win scholarships. At the age of
thirteen Gandhi married a girl of the same age who had been
chosen for him by his family, and the wedding ceremony has been
described as one of great pomp. Although his wife never learned
to speak the English in which Gandhi became fluent, and indeed
did not even learn to read, she was, nevertheless, a considerable
influence on him. There were four children born to this marriage.

Although Gandhi was born into the merchant caste of the
Hindu religion, he gave up that profession while studying law
in London. Law appealed to him, with the result that he made
high marks and was admitted to practice. While in London Gandhi
came under Christian influences which were to form his dominant
philosophy and determine the main activity of his life. He credited
Christianity with teaching him the principle of non-violence
which he was later to use as an invincible tool in liberating India
from British colonialism. Gandhi first used passive resistance in
South Africa, where he had gone for a court case. Seeing the
Hindu immigrants treated with gross injustice, and subjected to
deep prejudice, Gandhi spoke on their behalf, resulting in his imprisonment and his subsequent use of passive resistance to win
some freedoms for the Indians of South Africa. Gandhi remained
in South Africa for twenty-one years working for the rights of the

repressed Indians.

This activity inspired him to become a leader in the attempt to eliminate numerous ills which were then prevalent in his own land. Gandhi was stirred to anger by the utter squalor so evident everywhere in India. In addition, he was revolted by the caste system and the hopelessness of the masses who worked degrading jobs for a mere pittance. Gandhi saw, in the colonial policies of the British, the source of many bad laws and cruel injustices. The great desire of his heart, to which he was to dedicate the remainder of his life, was to attain freedom and independence for his people. And the great instrument to be used to gain this end was not a gun, but the practice of passive resistance.

Gandhi's efforts resulted in the refusal of his followers to hold any public office, along with a boycott of the courts and legislature, and of all foreign goods. As part of his campaign, Gandhi asked that children be withdrawn from the public schools. Though he knew it would be extremely difficult to attain, he also worked for peace between Hindus and Moslems. He took on the task of attempting to stop the trade in opium and in liquor, recognizing what these were doing to his people while the distributors grew wealthy. As he met the government head-on, especially in refusing to pay British taxes, he was imprisoned. But fearing his death as a martyr when he went on a hunger strike, the authorities released him. This alternating cycle of imprisonment and release was to be repeated a number of times, with Gandhi being arrested for his views and activities, then released when he went on a hunger strike. Always seeking justice, Gandhi would, surprisingly, work sometimes on behalf of the authorities who were imprisoning him. Those were the times when he was convinced that on some particular issue justice was on their side. As a result, he gained the respect of the British authorities and was awarded decorations by the British government. His reputation and his influence spread, also, by means of a weekly newspaper called, in English, *Indian Opinion,* which he edited.

To shorten the story of Gandhi's campaign for liberation, the end result was the granting, finally, of independence to India following World War II. Gandhi lived to enjoy his victory for only a short period of three years, when he was killed by an assassin's bullet. The killer was a misguided young man, fearful of Gandhi's tolerance for all creeds and religions, and who was himself a religious zealot. Gandhi was on his way to a prayer meeting at the time he was felled, and the whole world was in shock and mourning when this fanatic carried out his violent act in January of 1948. Burial was held in the tradition of Hindu cremation, though Gandhi had always acknowledged his debt to the Christian faith, especially in showing him the power of his chief weapon, passive resistance. As the father of his nation, he was honored with the term *Mahatma*, which means "the great soul."

Beyond freedom, Gandhi promoted social and economic reform. He disliked dissension and did not like to see his nation divided, so he tried to reconcile various religious groups in order to forestall strife and ill-will. But in seeking reconciliation, he refused to sacrifice the truth and reach agreement on the basis of the lowest common denominator. Instead, Gandhi sought the truth and tried to persuade others to see the rightness of his views. He called the truth "Satyagraha," and the term became a rallying cry. Gandhi sought to put values into true perspective by stressing behaviour over achievement. For Gandhi, being good was more important than being great. Thus, in all walks of life, one should live in good relations with one's fellow beings, not seeking advancement at the expense of others. A brave but gentle man, Gandhi did not even believe that animals should be killed, and was consistent in stressing non-violence; for instance, as leader of the Indian Nationalist Movement, when his campaign brought on a series of riots, Gandhi temporarily called off the campaign.

His remarkable ingenuity covered many fronts. For instance, he taught his followers to make salt out of sea water, defying the British Salt Acts which decreed that salt could be purchased only from the government — which added a heavy tax to the sale. To put people to work, he organized a program of hand weaving and spinning. This, he believed, not only gave people a chance for gainful occupation, but reduced the monopoly of the British textile industry. This diversity of talents has caused Gandhi to be described as a theologian, a lawgiver, a sanitary engineer, an authority on dialectics, a peacemaker, a salt-gatherer, and most certainly a statesman.

Of himself, Gandhi stated "Most religious men I have met are politicians in disguise. I, however, who wear the guise of a politician, am at heart a religious man." There is no doubt that he was a man for whom truth demanded the ultimate loyalty; it was to be followed regardless of cost. As a result, no one doubted Gandhi's sincerity and everyone knew he would cling to his course once he regarded it as right. Gandhi put full confidence in the ultimate victory of right over might, and of love over hate. He was humility personified. His modesty was clearly evident in his simple dress; he often went barefoot and always wore plain homespun garments. His humility was evident, too, as he worked with coolies on sugar plantations, or chose to travel third-class on the railways. He gave up a lucrative law practice, then turned over his personal finances to the founding of a new settlement, based on Tolstoy's principles. The settlement was located near Durban, where he adopted a life of poverty, believing it would give him the freedom to work for his fellow Indians. Here he spent more time on menial tasks than any others, and carried his simple approach to life into his eating habits. In accord with the teachings of his religion Gandhi was a strict vegetarian who, for long periods of time, ate only a single meal each day consisting of nuts and fruit, and whole-meal bread which he sometimes baked himself.

Jawaharlal Nehru once declared,

*His death brought more tributes than have ever been paid at the passing away of any other human being in history.*

He further described Gandhi in these words,

*His dominating passion was truth . . . That truth led him to fight evil and untruth wherever he found them, regardless of consequences. That truth made services to the poor and dispossessed the passion of his life, for where there is inequity and discrimination and supression there is injustice and evil and untruth. He taught us to rise above our little selves and prejudices and to see good in others . . . throughout his life he thought of India in terms of the poor and oppressed and downtrodden. To raise them and free them was the mission of his life. He adopted their ways of life and dress so that none in the country may feel lowly. Victory to him was the growth of freedom of these people."*

Einstein joined in the parade of praise by saying,

*"Generations to come, it may be, will scarce believe that such a one as this ever in flesh and blood walked upon this earth."*

Gandhi's liberation of India from the yoke of Great Britain has been described as a parallel to the liberation of the whole world from prejudice. He was a great teacher who taught by personal example and practice, and at times the tributes paid him were the highest compliments possible, as for instance, this statement by Viscount Louis Mount Batten, the last British Viceroy of India, who knew him well, "He will go down in history on a par with Buddha and Christ."

# Herbert Clark Hoover

(1874-1964)

The world fame and giant accomplishments of Herbert Hoover are made more dramatic by the humble beginnings from which he made his meteoric rise to international renown. Hoover was born into the family of a blacksmith, in the tiny village of West Branch, Iowa. His parents were Quakers of lower than middle-class standing, and he suffered the loss of both of them while he was still a child; Hoover was just six years old when he lost his father, and his mother passed away when he was only ten. Thereafter, he lived in a succession of homes, all of them with people of sturdy Quaker faith, who encouraged his adoption of a high standard of ethics and morality. The hardships of his youth continued into early manhood, and Hoover was able to attend college but only by working to pay his own way. He then began his adult life as a lowly laborer, immersed in the drudgery of a mine.

Hoover's mother had been a school teacher, whose "higher education" had consisted of only a couple years in the Preparatory Department of Iowa State University at Ames. Her professional experience was not lengthy, as she taught for only a brief time. But she unquestionably had considerable talent, especially in public speaking, for after her husband's death she was frequently called upon to speak in Quaker churches in Iowa. As a widow, she supported her three children by means of her ability as a seamstress.

The spirit and philosophy of the Hoover family is revealed, rather amusingly, by a statement made by Herbert's grandmother to one of his nieces. When the child, with some pride, came to her grandmother with the question, "Is it true that I am descended from John Wesley, the founder of the Methodist Church?" the grandmother's gruff reply was this, "Begone with thee! What matter if we be descended from the highest unless we are something ourselves. Get busy." Whether or not he, too, heard this wisdom, Herbert Hoover did get busy. As a lad he learned to hunt and fish and perform many chores around the house or in the nearby forest. In addition to this physical effort, Hoover also displayed a great hunger for learning. Though just an average student in his schoolwork at this time, he constantly sought for knowledge outside the classroom. He would ask questions of anyone who might enlighten him from their own background of specialized learning. A case in point is Hoover's study of geology under a dentist who took a great interest in stones, and who had accumulated quite a geological collection. Hoover was fascinated by the dentist's hobby and eagerly learned more about it. Perhaps this was the start of Hoover's real interest in mining, as he saw in it more than the mere drudgery of underground toil. It was characteristic of Hoover to learn from anyone around him who offered some new field of study. In his pre-college days, Hoover came into contact with people who typed, or knew bookkeeping, or blue-printing, and immediately learned from each of them the skill of his training. In addition Hoover possessed another asset, which he developed early in life — a rather phenominal memory, which was to give him a great advantage throughout his career.

Shortly after he entered his teens, Herbert went to Salem, Oregon to live with the family of his uncle, a Dr. John Minthorn. This provided many advantages, for in addition to his practice as a medical doctor, the physician was principal of the Friends Pacific Academy. Hoover studied at the Academy until, at the age of seventeen, he entered the newly established Stanford University. During his time at the Academy Hoover began the custom of performing odd jobs, in addition to his studies, in order to help meet his expenses. His time was further filled, and profitably, by night classes which he attended at a business school in Salem.

Hoover entered Stanford as a member of its first class, and immediately added odd jobs to his regimen. These included a laundry agency which he organized, collecting laundry on Monday and returning it on Friday. The enterprise eventually led to his hiring other students to help in the business. He delivered newspapers, also, and most importantly gained student employment in the Geology Department of the University.

Hoover's first real entry into the field of geology, which led him on into mining engineering, came from Dr. John Branner, who was then head of the Geology Department of the University.

Branner saw great possibilities in Hoover and he rewarded the young man's interest in this field by making the student his part-time secretary. Then, when the first school year ended, Branner secured a summer job for Hoover with the Geological Survey of the Ozarks, where the professor served as Arkansas State Geologist. Each summer thereafter Herbert learned more about his future profession by working with geological survey teams in various parts of the West. He graduated with two achievements outside scholarship, though he was successful in that area as well. One of these achievements was his reputation for being an outstanding student leader. The other was his courtship, later resulting in marriage, of Lou Henry, daughter of a banker in Monterey, California. A girl who majored in geology, she was a rarity in those days, and to Hoover's amazement she had been born in Iowa just four months after his birth.

Hoover certainly began his life career at the bottom. Jobs were scarce when he graduated, and so it was necessary to take any offering one was fortunate enough to secure. For Hoover, even with a university degree in engineering, this meant pushing a handcar as a laborer in a dark and damp mine in the Sierras. His daily wage for a ten-hour shift, usually during night hours, was two dollars. But he was a fast learner who drove himself to the utmost, and so he rose rapidly as his outstanding talents were recognized. In just a few years he was offered an invitation for a well-paying position from an outstanding London company, specializing as mining consultants. They immediately sent Hoover to Australia, where a gold rush had begun. There he rapidly established his reputation as one of the finest mining engineers, and his reputation spread, through mining journals, throughout the world. This brought Hoover great wealth, most of which he lost in paying off the debts of a partner who had swindled a million dollars, though Hoover owed no such obligation. But it took only a few years for Hoover to become even richer than he had been before. From Australia he moved in succession to highly responsible positions in Singapore, Burma, and Russia. Thus the boy from a small town in Iowa became familiar with the far-flung areas of the world. He was still fairly young when he had become managing director of not one but half a dozen companies doing business on every continent. Hoover was now known no longer as a boy wonder, but as "the great engineer."

On any honest rating of character, Hoover would receive the highest marks. He exhibited the height of his moral stature when he refused to allow drinking, swearing miners to alter his habits or speech. It can truly be said of Hoover that he was a states-man, not a politician. He brought dignity and honesty to the Presidency, when that high honor came to him, remaining free from any false promises or any compromise for personal benefit. Hoover refused to manipulate people or to let his personal accom-plishments be used for political gain. He admitted that he was not interested in personal power, and that he did not like superficial contacts. He utterly refused to enhance his political career by any compromise with evil, and was a man who simply could not hold a grudge nor retain bitterness toward even his worst detractors.

In dealing with problems, planning programs, and in work-ing with people, Hoover constantly thought in terms of moral-ity. The *Christian Century* praised his moral strength, and what they called his "spiritual grandeur," in his persistent drive to feed the hungry and save human lives on a grand and heroic scale, (in programs which will be described later). With the passing of time even his bitter enemies had to concede that he was, indeed, a man of steadfast honesty and deep humanitarianism.

Hoover also had no tolerance for fuzzy thinking, and insist-ed upon clarity of thought and logic, based on established fact. He never engaged in light talk or banter, but was an intellectual who turned to lightheartedness only within the family circle. He was a great philanthropist, but hid his generosity rather than receive appreciation or praise. His was a self-sacrificing character, and it can truly be said of Hoover that he carried no grudges, had no spirit of revenge, and found it easy to forgive, even when he was badly hurt by those who maligned him.

Hoover's Quaker faith left a strong and lasting impression on him, shaping his ideals as a boy and determining his character as a man. From his religion, he developed the philosophy that life should be taken seriously and that one must constantly hold a charitable attitude toward his fellows, offering service wherever needed. Indeed, Hoover believed that service to others was to be considered not a duty, done grudgingly or sparingly, but a privilege to be performed freely. This attitude would lead Hoover to plunge into welfare work on a gigantic scale, and to refuse compensation for his services outside his business responsibilities. He was taught that religion was a way of life, calling for utter honesty and fairness, and the sacredness of one's word. Indeed, he believed, one was born to serve, to practice self-discipline, and to suppress self-interest in a desire to be useful.

The strong imprint of his religion on Hoover's life and thought is apparent in his writing and speeches. Once, in addressing a meeting of the American Red Cross he declared, "It is indeed the spiritual in the individual and the nation which looks out with keen interest on the well-being of others, forgetful of ourselves, beyond our own preoccupation with our own selfish interests, and gives us a sense of belonging to the great company of mankind, sharing in the great plan of the universe and the definite order which pervades it."

At the age of forty Hoover became restless. He had firmly established a world-wide reputation as an engineer and had amassed considerable wealth. He had offices in ten cities scattered around the world, as well as one in New York and another in San Francisco. But he wanted his life to have more substance than material success and reputation could provide. He considered retiring and volunteering for public service; then suddenly a door opened that would lead Hoover out of engineering and into public life, where he was to give useful service for a number of decades.

World War I broke out, with all the social upheaval such a catastrophe brings. One such calamity was the pitiful plight of the people of Belgium. Germany had invaded that country and the British Navy was blockading it. This resulted in a complete cutoff of all food and a dearth of provisions essential for life. Widespread hunger increased quickly, becoming so severe that the attention of the world was attracted to the crisis. Hoover was selected as the one man who could bring various parties to agreement, organize a campaign, and so alleviate the situation. For eight years thereafter he was to serve as Chairman of the Commission for the Relief of Belgium, then as Food Administrator for the United States Government, as Executive Officer of the Supreme Economic Council of Paris, Manager for European Relief, and finally as the organizer of the effort to overcome famine in Russia. These were all massive efforts on Hoover's part, demanding tact and diplomacy, skill in reconciling various parties and nations, and the ability to secure food and distribute it efficiently. Through these efforts Hoover, for a second time, attained world wide recognition and various honors, though he always discouraged the bestowal of medals and ribbons. Still, they came, and in abundance. Because the Belgian government knew of Hoover's aversion to decorations, yet yearned to recognize his enormous contribution to their nation in its time of dire need, they bestowed upon him an unusual honor naming him "Citizen of the Belgian State and Friend of Belgian People."

Upon returning to his homeland Hoover began serving as an administrator within his own government. First President Harding, and then President Coolidge, selected him as Secretary of Commerce. From these cabinet appointments, Hoover advanced to the presidency himself, as the chief executive officer of our nation. In that high position, Hoover showed character and ingenuity; and his achievements were many. But a world wide depression devastated the American economy. In October 1929 the Stock Market crashed, and was followed by a period of mass unemployment. Mr. Hoover launched public works programs to put people back to work, won from Congress a reduction in income-tax rates, and called for a moratorium on debt. But the Depression was world wide and solutions were exasperatingly difficult. America was to feel its bite for a decade. Not until World War II put people to work in America's "arsenal for democracy," while millions of others joined the armed services, would the job market once again reach the point where those who wanted work could find it. The discontent of many, arising from the Depression, was seized upon with alacrity by a viciously unfair political machine which was thus able to limit Hoover's term in office to four years. He never accepted a dollar in salary during the time he carried the heavy burdens of the nation. Fortunately, he lived long enough to see the tide of hatred, spawned by those who later admitted there had been libel for political gain, turn once again in his favor.

The completion of his term as the thirty-first president of the United States did not end Hoover's distinguished public service. Two of his successors in office made use of his outstanding talents. From 1946 to 1949 Hoover headed various commissions appointed by President Truman. From 1953 to 1955 he served as chairman of a commission appointed by President Eisenhower, charged with the weighty responsibility of reorganizing the federal government. At the age of eighty, in an address delivered at his birthplace, Hoover credited two sources as well-springs of hope for the future of his beloved country. As an engineer, he mentioned the creative ability of Americans. As the voice of a man deeply devoted to his faith, he pointed to "Religious devotion."

The meanness and bitterness with which his political detractors painted him, erased the true picture of Hoover during the years when the world was heading towards its calamitous depression. He was one of the most outrageously maligned men ever to be purposely misjudged by those who sought to advance their own political ends through smearing another's name. They wanted to guarantee that the public did not see a president carrying unusually heavy burdens, enduring exceedingly long hours of work, handicapped by endless opposition from maneuvering politicians. They tried to cover up his world renown, to erase the name of Hoover Dam, and make him the scapegoat of the faulty world economy by referring for years to the "Hoover depression." Hoover's refusal to show resentment, even though deeply hurt, or to strike back at his detractors, was a singular mark of this man's virtuous character.

No one else can match Hoover's great deeds, saving millions of Frenchmen and Belgians, and tens of millions of others scattered widely throughout Europe, from famine and pestilence; reorganizing the greatest government in the world, saving vast mining empires, and feeding whole continents. For these and other accomplishments Hoover was highly honored throughout the world, as few people have ever been. In a great many cities there are streets bearing his name. Poland erected a statue as tribute to him. Cities striking medals in his honor numbered several dozen. And as already stated, Belgium gave him the status of "citizen and friend of Belgium." He was widely known to be the organizer and leader in the rehabilitation of a war-torn world lying in ruins.

If Hoover were not so well known for outstanding achievement in several other fields, he would have been remembered in American history as a first-rate author and writer. The books he published range over a wide scope of topics, some historical, some scholarly and philosophical, some the result of special executive talents, others dealing with fishing or the art of growing up. Let a few of his titles speak for themselves: *Addresses Upon the American Road, Basis of Lasting Peace, Challenge to Liberty,*

*Principles of Mining, Memoirs, Fishing For Fun, On Growing Up, Ordeal of Woodrow Wilson,* and *Commission on Organization of the Executive Branch of Government.* In addition, Hoover's scholarship was such that, with his well-educated wife, he translated from Latin the pioneer work of Agricola, *De re Metallica,* a prodigious task which other scholars had thought too difficult to translate.

Herbert Hoover spent the last two decades of his life in New York City, where he died in 1964, at the age of ninety, retaining his mental alertness until the end. Funeral services were conducted in New York City and in Washington, D.C., with burial near his birthplace in West Branch, Iowa.

# James Cash Penney

(1875-1971)

J. C. Penney's early life gave no promise of his future as a man whose name would be well known throughout the United States. He grew up on a small farm in Kentucky, the son of a minister of the Primitive Baptist Church. Both parents were devout and impressed their children with their sturdy trust in God and their lives of prayer. The father was determined to raise his children to be self-reliant, and perhaps carried this ideal to an extreme when he forced his eight-year-old son, James, to pay for all his clothes. The lad was thus forced to do what work he could on the farm, attempting to raise pigs for a profit, as well as to mow lawns and run erands. The father had a purpose in dealing so rigorously with his children, for he wanted them to learn honesty, integrity, moral and ethical values, and consideration for others. He imbued in them, also, a rejection of self-pity, and a willingness to learn a lesson from every mistake or misfortune. His son, James, learned these lessons well. As part of his religious development James attended neighboring Sunday church schools twice each Sunday with his brother, once at a Baptist and once at a Presbyterian church. About this time, the father was ousted from his ministerial office, which further increased the family's difficulty in making ends meet. As a result of financial stringency James began, while in his early teens, to work as a clerk in a local store. Though he did not realize it, this was the start for him of an illustrious career as a merchant — though there would first be some setbacks. Because his health was not good at this time, a doctor advised Penney to seek employment that would be less confining than working inside a store all day. So, in search of new employment, he headed for Denver, Colorado. But inability to find other work forced him once again to become a clerk in a dry goods store. Here, in spite of the doctor's advice, Penney came to the conclusion that since he enjoyed the work so much, his future must lie in this type of business activity. In Denver Penney was impresseed, also, by the opportunities and methods of chain store operation, an idea that was still in its infancy. The man for whom he worked owned stores in six different communities. Penney learned, also, the advantages of expanding on the basis of a business partnership rather than investing alone. His start as a partner in business began when he was sent to open and manage a store in Kemmerer, Wyoming. He was loaned the money to purchase a one-third interest in the enterprise. This generous offer amazed him, but it brought about some definite results. Penney was by nature a hard worker, but he realized that he was now spending many extra hours at the business due to his direct share in its results. He and his wife now worked almost night and day to make the business prosper. Now the influence of Penney's parents bacame evident, when he determined to stress honesty and to call his enterprise "The Golden Rule Store." This title is indicative of one of the strongest motivations and beliefs in Penney's life. He liked to persuade others that the living of this rule was of practical value in all phases of everyday life, the rule became his motto in life and in business. But he went still further, stressing clean morality and a Christian type of life for himself and all his employees.

Penney did not waste much time in making a good profit in this Kemmerer store, nor did he delay in expanding, for he opened two other stores on a partnership basis, and in a few years, bought out the others so that he became sole owner of all three stores. This was the start of bigger things, for the number kept growing, and with increasing speed, ultimately reaching the amazing figure of 1700, spread over forty-eight of the fifty States.

In the first years of his sojourn in Kemmerer, Penney developed a set of principles which not only proved successful in business, but which reveal the character of the man and the way he both selected his associates and trained his employees — two factors in his success. The six principles which he emphasized were: preparation wins; hard work wins; honesty wins; confidence in people wins; the spirit wins; a practical application of the Golden Rule wins. Penney knew that to many people these would sound old fashioned and trite, but he had such faith in their truth and practicality that he made them the foundation of his business enterprise. Time would prove how right he was, as his business spread throughout the United States and he became extremely wealthy.

The growth of the Penney enterprise came about not only on the basis of his business principles but also through a prodigious amount of labor on the part of both Mr. Penney and his wife, Berta. She was of inestimable help to him, and helped them to get by frugally during the early years of their marriage, when they were trying to get a start in the business world. She did not complain about his extra long hours, often seven days a week, which he gave to the business. And she helped him in the store in addition to managing the home. By the time Mr. Penney was thirty-five, they had begun to meet with success and could look with satisfaction at their chain of fourteen stores. Then suddenly tragedy struck. What was expected to be a minor operation for the removal of Berta Penney's tonsils proved fatal. Mr. Penney was on a business trip at the time, and the shock of her unexpected death overwhelmed him. Left with two young sons, feeling lonely and depressed, he was seemingly unable to handle his grief. At times, on business trips to New York Penney would walk the streets at night until exhausted, in order to fall asleep when he retired. Gradually, the passing of time and his faith restored his peace of mind, and he was able to proceed once more with business and family affairs. But this acceptance came only after two or three years, during which time a clergy friend, Dr. Short, proved to be beneficial.

The religious faith which enabled Penney to overcome his grief was a dominant factor throughout his life. Raised as he was in a strictly religious home, this influence stayed with him always. Late in life, when he wrote his autobiography, he dedicated it to a friend whom he described as "a life which was a sure sign of that New Life in Christ, which endures." In speaking of the men he selected to help him run his business, Penney once wrote, "I never hired anyone who did not have a positive belief in a Supreme Being." He was determined to build his business on a foundation which was ethical and moral. True to his upbringing, he was a strong believer in prayer, not just at certain times, but throughout the day as the Spirit moved him. It was a powerful factor in developing his spiritual realtionship with God. Penney referred to prayer as a business companion, and he encouraged intercessory prayer.

Among Penney's recorded statements is this, "A full understanding of life is impossible without love of God." He also wrote,

*Laymen have a privileged obligation to the church. Rich is our spiritual heritage and we all owe more than we can repay in our span of life to the church . . . It is the layman's great opportunity to give himself, his talents, experience and support to the church. In turn the church has to offer an ever-growing opportunity for spiritual growth of the layman through helping him to see the privilege of bridging the gap between the practical and the spiritual.*

Penney was greatly influenced by the concept of the brotherhood of man, declaring that we do not work hard enough in attempting to achieve it, and considering it a sacred trust from Christ that we should work for the spread of this concept and ideal. He liked to use the phrase "Family of Man," urging prayer for larger understanding and sympathy with one's fellow creatures.

There were many facets to J. C. Penney's dreams apart from his efforts as an outstanding merchandiser and chain store owner. For instance, though he had little formal education, Penney was quick to admit the fact and to do something about it. Realizing that his written communications were open to considerable criticism in their use of grammar and punctuation, he hired a man of considerable talent in that field to take over this area of management within his company. But he wanted to be of help to people in his company, thus increasing their efficiency, so he instructed this man, Dr. Thomas Tapper, to set up a reading and study course for the improvement of Penney employees. First, however, Penney subjected himself to a tutoring course under this able teacher. Over a period of eighteen months, for half of each business day, Penney studied diligently at reading and writing, and became acquainted with the great intellectual leaders of history. He was determined to develop himself as a speaker and writer in order to meet the many requests now coming to him for interviews and speeches as one of the nation's outstanding businessmen. The first attempt to introduce his employees to education and culture took the form of a monthly periodical called *The Dynamo*. It was his awareness of the weaknesses in this publication that led him to hire Dr. Tapper. *The Dynamo* was soon supplanted by the *Store Meeting Manual*, outlining all phases of successful employees meetings within each store, in order to develop them and improve their ability to handle their particular responsibilities. Later, Penney persuaded his long-time ministerial friend, Dr. Short, to join with Dr. Tapper in this public relations area, where they proved to be highly complementary to each other. Dr. Short would give public lectures on the Penney Principles in various cities, where by now more than three hundred stores were located. Thus, with publications and speeches, this venture became a good-sized educational program.

His productive mind led Mr. Penney to involvement in another, quite different, venture, as well. He had always felt drawn to agriculture and to the breeding of fine cattle. Meeting a strong urge to improve cattle breeding in the United States, an area in which our nation was then far behind certain European countries, Penney purchased 750 acres of farm land in New York State, bought some highly pedigreed cattle, and selected an expert in animal husbandry to run the operation of a breeding farm. Penney arranged for the University of Missouri to be the final recipient of this successful operation by willing that in 1996 the estate should be given to that University as an adjunct to its department of agriculture. But this farm was only the beginning. Penney received much satisfaction from becoming one of America's leading breeders of pure-bred cattle, and in watching the dairy herds of America improve because of his efforts.

He soon followed the New York venture with the purchase of 120,000 acres of land in Florida. Twenty thousand acres had been cleared of timber, and on that acreage Penney brought a new idea to reality. He carefully selected farmers, most of whom had been brought to his attention through his store managers, and helped them to settle on this land. They were, like the store managers, to be partners in a large corporate effort. He made it easy, financially, for the farmers to gain ownership of the tract of land assigned to them, and stocked the land with three thousand range cattle, in addition to swine and pure-bred poultry, numbering four thousand. He brought in as heads of the operation two experienced and capable educators; one was the former dean of the Oregon School of Commerce and the other had headed the Vocational Department at Berea College in Kentucky. Through this program Penney not only aided individual farmers, but was also responsible for agricultural advancement in the United States.

Another educational adventure for Penney was the result of an idea which had been slowly developing in his mind for some time. Its purpose was to give vocational and spiritual guidance to young people. As usual, Mr. Penney translated his idea into action by selecting a talented individual to implement it. The idea was to help spread the teachings and ideals of Christ among young people as a guide and motivation in their developing lives. The man chosen to make the idea a reality was the well-known Baptist minister, Dr. Daniel Poling. Penney established a foundation which provided the means for Dr. Poling to present a radio program known as the National Youth Conference. Each Sunday afternoon, several hundred young people would gather together at the Waldorf Astoria Hotel in New York City. Dr. Poling would speak on the teachings of Jesus, and questions and discussion on the part of the young people followed. The entire program was broadcast by radio, at first over one station and ultimately over a chain of thirty-eight, reaching a large number of youth.

As a result of this contact with Dr. Poling, Penney's foundation underwrote much of the cost of publishing the *Christian Herald*, which Dr. Poling edited. It was a magazine attractive to Penney because of its interdenominational appeal, reaching into thousands of American homes, offering guidance and inspiration as a Christian publication. Penney wanted to be a contributing factor in what he considered an effective means of Christian education.

While living in New York City Mr. Penney became actively involved in a weekly meeting of businessmen who came together for prayer at an Episcopal church. He was thus inspired to read and study about prayer and our personal relationship with God. He joined the Laymen's Movement for a Christian World and became a speaker on behalf of the Movement in widespread cities. Penney thus became vitally interested in the proposition that one could be a success in the business world and at the same time a devout Christian. He made speeches on this subject in travels around the country, coming to the conclusion that a full understanding of life is possible only through love of God. Penney declared that our nation cannot fulfill its destiny without the vitalizing force of the Christian home.

When the Great Depression struck the United States, it came at a time when Mr. Penney was vulnerable. He had been adding outside interests to his chain store business and some of these were proving to be extremely costly. He had borrowed heavily in order to establish some of these various enterprises, and he had been most generous in giving financial help to organizations and individuals. The Depression prompted the banks to request the return of his loans sooner than Penney had expected, further tightening the noose around his financial neck. But he and his financial consultants proved equal to the task, and by reducing the number of his various interests, Penney rode out the Depression, returning to the task of expanding the chain of Penney stores. They grew to number 1700 and covered forty-eight states. Once again, he was established as one of the great merchants and businessmen of America, as well as one of its great philanthropists.

J. C. Penney passed away at an advanced age, able to look back on a long, varied, and interesting career in which he had been able to help numerous worthwhile causes. And he could proudly accept the laudatory title of outstanding Christian businessman.

# Marian Anderson

(1902-        )

Marian Anderson, the first black woman to become a star in the concert world, rose from humble beginnings to become a performer of world-wide acclaim. And from the start of her interest in music, as a young girl, to the pinnacle of success, religion played an important part in her life and in her magnificent achievements.

Her birth could not have been much more lowly. When her parents married, they rented a single room in south Philadelphia, and with the arrival of Marian, the three-member family lived in that single room. Later, the family moved to larger quarters out of the necessity to accomodate an enlarging circle that included three daughters.

There was always music in the home, as the youthful daughters, even before they attended school, would sing together. A strongly religious family, their music consisted largely of hymns and spirituals. As a faithful attendant at Union Baptist Church, Marian was early admitted to the junior choir, and the first public performance of her life was as a member of a duet, singing at a service in her church. Later she progressed to the senior choir, where her unusual talents were obvious and she was given recognition as an outstanding soloist.

It was through her church that she, as a young girl, met the renowned Roland Hayes, who had established the custom of presenting a concert once a year at Union Baptist Church. This great performer not only helped Marian by making important suggestions concerning her singing, but by opening engagements for her as well. Thus, her reputation spread, and she began singing in various churches and at other public events.

But, Anderson's climb to greatness was not easy. For instance, the money for singing lessons was scarce. To her credit, she plodded along on her own initiative, and it was the recognition of her talent by her home congregation, and the willingness of its members to come to her support, that led to her first lessons with the accomplished teacher, Guiseppe Boghetti. Completely unable to pay the considerable price of her lessons, she learned that the Union Baptists had set out to raise the funds to secure this special training for her.

Marian faced disappointment and apparent set-backs on several occasions, such as the first time she sang at Town Hall in New York. The audience was disappointing, and to make matters worse, the newspaper critics were devasting. In her bitter disappointment, she was supported and uplifted by her mother, a woman of deep spirituality and much prayer. The mother's encouraging words to her daughter included the advice to, "Pray about it." It was also her saintly mother who often repeated to her daughter the admonition, "Grace comes before greatness." So it came to be that Marian's inspiration to rise from periods of despair was the belief that she had God-given talents and that God intended for her to use those abilities with which he had endowed her. So, she sallied forth against great odds, confident that God would direct her path and watch over her. She gave him the glory and retained a humble attitude, even when her fame had grown world-wide. She would take breaks in her schedule to sing for other humble people when opportunities arose for helping a worthy cause, and she remained, always, less interested in the money than in the proper stewardship of her talents. This dedication of her services to God's call was a dominant factor in her ability to impress audiences and charge them with emotion, as she sang such familiar hymns as *Were You There When They Crucified My Lord?*, *He's Got The Whole World In His Hand*, or *Go Down Moses.*

In every concert she gave her best whether the audience was large or small, and many a worthy cause benefitted from a concert where she donated her performance. Hospitals, prisons, army camps overseas, all were lifted in spirit by her unselfish services. The strength of her religious convictions show clearly in her autobiography, *My Lord, What a Morning,* and in her attitude toward life. She once told some school children, "Things like hate and fear destroy you, restrict you from being the kind of big person you could be." Those who have known her best are convinced, and do not hesitate to say, that the main reason for Miss Anderson's success has been her trust in God and her confidence that he will ultimately make everything turn out right.

Marian's interest in Negro spirituals was not based on the simple tie they represented with her forebears, for she saw in them the deepest expressions of the emotions and spiritual conceptions of her culture. She has told of her trip to the Holy Land when she visited so many places mentioned in the Bible, including Gethsemane, the Mount of Olives, the shores of the Dead Sea, and the River Jordan. But, while she was thrilled to be visiting such holy places, the trip had been somewhat disillusioning for her; she had been led to imagine these places to be much larger than they actually were. When she had sung "The River Jordan is so wide, I don't know how to get to the other side," she had pictured in her mind a mighty river with a great expanse from shore to shore. Again, the spiritual, "Joshua fit the battle of Jericho," had given her a mental image of great, towering battle-ments. But, alas, the remnants of the walls of Jericho were far from impressive, while the River Jordan turned out to be both narrow and muddy. Then, she said it struck her that her ances-tors, tied down and bound in slavery, had grasped at the stories contained in the Bible, and used them as a basis from which to let their imaginations soar, picturing freedom and blessings denied them in their servitude and drudgery. Their souls had been given freedom to rise in the spiritual songs which came out of Scrip-ture. The spirituals they had created had met some of their deepest emotional needs.

In speaking of her own religious commitment, Marian said that religion is something to be cherished, and that even though she could not attend church every Sunday she was concerned that she be on good speaking terms with her Creator. She declared,

> I believe that I could not have had my career without the help of the Being above. I believe, as mother does, that He put it in the hearts of many people to be kind, interested and helpful, and to do things that needed to be done for me and that I could not have done for myself. It would have happened anyhow, some people might say. I don't believe that it would have happened anyhow.

She credited her mother with planting the seeds of faith in her heart, and for Marian, her mother serves as an example of how one should meet life and face its hardships, trusting in the Lord for his guidance, help and inspiration.

As she achieved some degree of fame, Marian began attracting to her church many people who came just to hear this remarkable young girl sing. It may come as a surprise, but voice was not Marian's only musical interest. When she was very small she would dream that a bench in the kitchen was a piano and she would go through the motions of playing it. The violin greatly appealed to her also. Her father, knowing how much she longed for one, managed to save enough pennies out of his hard-earned dollars to buy a cheap instrument. She was only eight years old when this event became the highlight of her life. The playing of the violin did not last, but later she reveled in a real piano.

At the age of eight Marian sang for religious services in a vacant store which had been turned into a temporary place of worship. The pastor found her to be such a drawing card that he even advertised her as a "baby contralto" whom people should attend his services to hear.

The help of friends during her youthful years of poverty was a great factor in developing Marian's musical talents. For almost a year she received free lessons in voice from Mary Saunders Patterson, who recognized the girl's immense possibilities. Later, the Philadelphia Choral Society gave a benefit concert which provided her with a two-year scholarship to study under Agnes Reimsnyder. And, as noted previously the Union Baptist Church organized a benefit concert to provide money for her music lessons.

But as Marian's training progressed, she developed a great desire to study under Guiseppe Boghetti, a well-known and widely-respected vocal teacher in Philadelphia and New York. She finally managed to secure an interview with him, but just when he had experienced an unusually busy and tiring day. Late in the afternoon, he reluctantly gave Marian an audition. In spite of his weariness, and the chore of listening to yet another aspirant, Boghetti admitted her to his studio. But he quickly recovered from his ennui when he heard her sing. As she sang "Deep River," tears came to his eyes and he gladly accepted her as a pupil. It was under his guidance that she won a competition to serve as soloist with the Philadelphia Symphony Orchestra in the Lewisohn Stadium in New York. Later she won the Julius Rosenwald Scholarship at a concert in Carnegie Hall, New York.

Anderson then went to Europe, where her fame soared like an eagle. Germany received her with great ovations. And a manager in Sweden sent a Finnish pianist to Germany to scout her talents. He not only gave such a favorable report that she was invited to Sweden where her ovations continued, but Mr. Vehanen, the Finnish pianist who sent the report, became her accompanist. Then followed the final sprint to glory. Marian began singing in the largest and best known music halls throughout Europe, Russia, and America. It became common for box offices to post the "Sold Out" sign well ahead of her appearances.

But fame did not diminish the religious fervor of Miss Anderson. She would not hesitate to announce "I do a good deal of praying," and she has been well described as "ardently religious." She always included the Negro spirituals of her youth in her repertoire, saying "Spirituals are my own music." But she loved them not only because of their identity with her history but because of their deeply moving religious messages. Marian Anderson could aptly be called a "musical missionary to the world."

# Dag Hammarskjold

(1905-1961)

This outstanding, international statesman was born in Jonkoping, Sweden, on July 29, 1905. It is said that his mother, after giving birth to three children, all boys, had hoped that her fourth child would be a girl, and was therefore disappointed at his birth. Yet, in later years, she was not only thrilled by Dag's great accomplishments, but enjoyed an especially close relationship to this son. Because he never married, he remained at home with her for thirty-five years, thus affording them a close companionship. This relationship was important, for it was his mother's deep pietism, with its emphasis on spiritual and moral qualities, which resulted in Dag's spiritual emphasis as a statesman. He once declared that "from scholars and clergymen on my mother's side I inherited a belief that, in the very radical sense of the Gospels, all men were equal as children of God, and should be met and treated by us as our masters in God." There is no doubt that his mother's pietism made a strong impression upon Dag. Once he was asked which he considered the three most indispensable books for a person to know. He answered that his choice would be the Bible, *Shakespeare's Collected Works,* and *Don Quixote.*

In addition to his mother, a second principal influence moulding Dag's philosophy of life was Albert Schweitzer's ideal of love for humanity. He once asked the question, "Where is there human warmth?" and his own answer was, "In any situation it is, I suppose, part of the price of what one does that you can give yourself as unreservedly as is possible . . . The compensation is the bright-light warmth I possess in contact with my friends, a sort of comradeship beneath the same stars, in which one does not ask and receives so much." He paid tribute to Albert Schweitzer by writing, "The two ideals which dominated my childhood world met me fully harmonized and adjusted to the demands of our world of today in the ethics of Albert Schweitzer, where the ideal of service is supported by, and supports, the basic attitude to man set forth in the Gospels."

Among Hammarskjold's writings are statements defining such religious subjects as faith. He writes:

> Faith is a state of the mind and soul. In this sense we can understand the word of the Spanish mystic, Saint John of the Cross: "Faith is the union of God with the soul." The language of religion is a set of formulas which register a basic spiritual experience. It must not be regarded as describing in terms to be defined by philosophy, the reality which is accessible to our senses and which we analyze with the tools of logic. I was late in understanding what this meant. When I finally reached that point, the beliefs in which I was once brought up and which, in fact, had given my life direction even while my intellect still challenged their validity, were recognized by me as mine in their own right and by my free choice. I feel that I can endorse these convictions without any compromise with the demands of that intellectual honesty which is the very key to maturity of mind."

In preparing for a brilliant career, Dag displayed, during his years of formal education, a keen and discerning mind. His rise to fame was unbelievably fast. Because of his scholastic record, he was selected to teach political economy at Stockholm University, though somewhat young for this position. Having been influenced for life by his mother's spiritual ideals, the influence of his father now became clear in Dag's life. His father had once served as Prime Minister of Sweden, and it was really no surprise that Dag should become interested in public service. Thus, at the early age of thirty-one he was appointed the Undersecretary of the Ministry of Finance. Five years later, at the age of thirty-six, Hammarskjold became the youngest chairman of the Bank of Sweden in its history. He was led into public service by his conviction that such service was the duty owed by every citizen. For him, public service in his own nation and throughout the world was the only means by which many international problems could be faced and conquered. For him it was a spiritual campaign filled with practical results.

Heading the nation's bank was not his only form of public service. From time to time he was called upon to apply his talents to various other positions of great importance, including Financial

Advisor to the Foreign Minister, and Vice-Minister of Foreign Affairs — positions which gave him excellent experience for his future leadership of the United Nations. Hammarskjold's diplomatic experience outside his native land included service as a delegate to the Organization for European Economic Cooperation, membership in the Council of Europe, and a seat as delegate to the United Nations. In 1953 he was appointed as chair of Sweden's United Nation's delegation, and just one year later, became known throughout the world when he was chosen to succeed Trygve Lie as the second secretary general of the U. N. At the time of Hammarskjold's selection, his predecessor said to him, "You are taking over the world's most impossible job." When he had been in office for approximately seven years, a Swedish journalist, with that statement in mind, asked Hammarskjold whether he still retained the optimism with which he undertook his position. And Dag replied — "If I hadn't believed in (the office's) possibilities I wouldn't have stayed here."

His optimism did not prevent Hammerskjold from seeing the reality of his problems. He once declared to a friend that the world is a bit mad. He admitted that he yearned for "good, wise friends in some quiet corner, where you don't listen to the radio and are more interested in the migrant birds that now . . . have gone back to the Nile and its frogs." He sometimes referred to the ominous problems of the world. For instance, upon the death of a Swedish writer whom he admired, he paid his friend this tribute,

*He was one of the few, perhaps last, representatives of that spiritual superiority with its natural dignity, warm heart and unshakeable integrity, that is needed more than ever in this time of growing darkness and corruption.*

One of his early efforts in office was to seek an easing of the tension existing between the United States and the Soviet Union. He sometimes went beyond diplomacy, finding it necessary to use military power to ensure peace. Thus, in 1956 he helped create the U. N. army with members from twenty-one countries, numbering 19,000 troops, to control civil war in the Congo.

In his leadership of the U. N. Hammerskjold was known as an indefatigable worker, who spent long hours every day at his tasks, took no holidays, and worked on week-ends. His subordinates complained that he was apt to call them at any hour of the day or night and put them to work on a pressing problem, demanding that the work be completed without delay. His administration was a highly centralized one, and he kept in close touch with all phases of U. N. activities. But at the same time, he delegated considerable responsibilities to his chief officers, yet always with the expectation that they keep him well informed.

Hammarskjold's executive style was one which he called "quiet diplomacy." Though sometimes faced with knotty problems in his attempts to unite disagreeing parties, he proved to be successful in reaching his goals. His quiet diplomacy brought disputing parties together without publicity, then, in a face-to-face discussion of their differences, accomplished their reconciliation. In 1955 Hammarskjold visited Peking to discuss the release by the Chinese of eleven United States airmen, returning home triumphant in his mission.

Dag's service was made difficult by many problems which were constantly arising in the Congo and the Middle East. It was while working on a peace settlement in the Congo, while enroute to Kalanga, that his plane crashed and his eight year tenure in office came to an abrupt end. The entire world mourned over its loss, and his world peacemaking efforts were recognized when he was posthumously awarded the Nobel Peace Prize.

Dag Hammarskjold was a deeply religious man. He gave much time and thought to many of the spiritual aspects of life. The last book that he read was Thomas a Kempis's *The Imitation of Christ.* He had the highest of ideals, which he applied in a practical manner to life. His high standards are evidenced in his statement that intellectual honesty is the very key to maturity of mind. In his attempt to apply his spiritual ideals to life in this world, Hammarskjold drove himself relentlessly, seeking to make the United Nations the means whereby the world could be freed from poverty and war. It was in a sense as a martyr to his cause that he perished in the plane crash while serving as Secretary General. In addition to the spiritual and moral imprint which Hammerskjold left on his office, he also left behind a noble revelation of his spiritual concerns in his posthumously published (and widely acclaimed) work, *Markings.*

For Hammarskjold, his religion demanded its application to life, and so he said, "In our era, the road to holiness necessarily passes through the world of action." He believed that God was the single source from which one received the power to live life victoriously. He pointed to the basic human need for faith in God when he stated "God does not die on the day when we cease to believe in a personal deity, but we die on the day when our lives cease to be illuminated by the steady radiance, renewed daily, of a wonder, the source of which is beyond all reason."

He revealed in his writings and speeches an extensive knowledge of the Scriptures, with many remarks based on biblical characters and quotes. His *Markings* replete with many references to God and faith, revealing his own solid trust in his Creator, and a desire to let all of life be under divine direction. In fact, for Hammarskjold, life and God were completely interwoven. He was so impressed by the presence of God in one's personal life that he explained his own life's motivation by paraphrasing Saint Paul's famous statement, declaring "Not I, but God in me." This, for him, was the true source of inner strength, of his inspiration, and of his attainments. Thus, Hammarskjold is among the most recent to achieve true greatness through spiritual strength, an example of a vital godliness that truly changed the world.

# Postscript

There is much more that could be written about each of the people discussed within the preceeding pages. Libraries contain hundreds of volumes describing each of their exploits. These sketches of famous men and women are brief, but sufficient to introduce the reader to their subjects' achievements, and to the religious compulsion which each one displayed. The intent of the authors is to call attention to those who are described here in the hope that the reader will feel impelled to secure lengthier biographies and thus learn more about these famous and exciting lives.

To read about these people is to be inspired to develop one's own capabilities. Many of these twenty-two rose up out of poverty, some had very little formal education, and some even suffered serious health problems which plagued them throughout their lives. Yet each persevered, and came to be numbered among the great ones of this earth.

In learning about these people, one is struck by the recurrent influence of the home in their lives. It was in the home, and usually from their mother, that most of these men and women learned of religious and moral values, and their applications to everyday living. Such influence has an amazing way of turning up when least expected.

In the closing days of his life, Alfred Steinmetz, the great electrical wizard and inventor, was asked what he thought would be the next great discovery of mankind. His answer was surprising. Although he was a man who had forsaken his spiritual heritage and had disavowed religious belief, his reply revealed his return to the influence of his home. Looking to the possibilities of the future, he ignored the emerging discoveries of atomic power and planetary exploration. Instead he declared that the next great discovery of man would be in the realm of the spiritual. It was his conviction that when humanity uncovered the power that lies in the spiritual realm, more progress would be made in a single generation than in all the preceding years of life on earth.

Each new generation can profit from a knowledge of its predecessors who deserve admiration for their character and achievements. And on a wider scale, there is a need for citizens to learn of the benefits which religion brings to society as a whole, and to review the impact which religion had on our nation during its formative years. Perhaps such a review is more important today than ever, in light of the current world situation. For instance, it is sobering to hear what a man like Aleksandr Solzhenitsyn has to say. Viewing the tumultuous revolutions like the one that has shaken Russia, and witnessing the inhumanity that is rampant today, he declares that our current troubles are due to the fact that we have forgotten God. He staunchly believes that the outstanding trait of the twentieth century is humankind's alienation from God, and that the cure for society's present ills lies in the restoration of our lost religious faith. For Solzhenitsyn, hope lies in the fact that materialistic communism, which hates religion with a vengeance, as its declared number-one enemy, has shown that it cannot conquer Christianity.

When the awful horrors of World War II came to an end, General Douglas MacArthur stated that the solution to ending wars was theological. We need to ponder what he meant by that. Recently, Britain's Prince Charles, speaking at Harvard University's 350th anniversary celebration, challenged educators to emphasize moral education along with technical training. He stressed the need, in teaching people how to make things, to produce, as well, the kind of people who will exercise moral control over the things that they make. He further called upon parents to teach their children that they must have standards to live by. And he declared, also, that for too long we have lived dangerously in rejecting the most fundamental traditions of our Greek, Roman and Jewish inheritances.

A study of the lives included here confirms a belief in the extreme importance of the spiritual element as an ingredient of successful living. These people are among the "cloud of witnesses" whose example can arouse the spark that ignites human souls to strive for greatness. They all saw this world as one that can be enriched by the light of eternal truth. They tell us that God is ever available to enflame common lives with his shining presence.